CAMBRIDGE LIBRARY COLLECTION

Books of enduring scholarly value

British and Irish History, Seventeenth and Eighteenth Centuries

The books in this series focus on the British Isles in the early modern period, as interpreted by eighteenth- and nineteenth-century historians, and show the shift to 'scientific' historiography. Several of them are devoted exclusively to the history of Ireland, while others cover topics including economic history, foreign and colonial policy, agriculture and the industrial revolution. There are also works in political thought and social theory, which address subjects such as human rights, the role of women, and criminal justice.

Memoirs of Mrs Fitzherbert

Maria Fitzherbert (1756–1837) was already twice widowed when the young Prince of Wales began his pursuit of her in 1784. Initially refusing his offer of marriage, she eventually accepted it and the couple were wed in secret the following year. Though legitimate in her eyes, the union was invalid under the Royal Marriages Act of 1772, and controversial because of her Catholicism. A posthumous attack on her faith and morals, penned by Lord Holland in his *Memoirs of the Whig Party*, provoked her close friend Charles Langdale (1787–1868) into publishing this defence in 1856. A champion of Catholic emancipation, Langdale was one of the first Catholics elected to Parliament. These memoirs are based on Maria Fitzherbert's own recollections, recounted to Langdale's brother, Lord Stourton. They reveal the values and beliefs of an exceptional woman who occupied a unique and precarious position within British high society.

Cambridge University Press has long been a pioneer in the reissuing of out-of-print titles from its own backlist, producing digital reprints of books that are still sought after by scholars and students but could not be reprinted economically using traditional technology. The Cambridge Library Collection extends this activity to a wider range of books which are still of importance to researchers and professionals, either for the source material they contain, or as landmarks in the history of their academic discipline.

Drawing from the world-renowned collections in the Cambridge University Library and other partner libraries, and guided by the advice of experts in each subject area, Cambridge University Press is using state-of-the-art scanning machines in its own Printing House to capture the content of each book selected for inclusion. The files are processed to give a consistently clear, crisp image, and the books finished to the high quality standard for which the Press is recognised around the world. The latest print-on-demand technology ensures that the books will remain available indefinitely, and that orders for single or multiple copies can quickly be supplied.

The Cambridge Library Collection brings back to life books of enduring scholarly value (including out-of-copyright works originally issued by other publishers) across a wide range of disciplines in the humanities and social sciences and in science and technology.

Memoirs of Mrs Fitzherbert

With an Account of her Marriage with H.R.H. the Prince of Wales, Afterwards King George IV

CHARLES LANGDALE

CAMBRIDGE
UNIVERSITY PRESS

CAMBRIDGE UNIVERSITY PRESS

Cambridge, New York, Melbourne, Madrid, Cape Town,
Singapore, São Paolo, Delhi, Mexico City

Published in the United States of America by Cambridge University Press, New York

www.cambridge.org
Information on this title: www.cambridge.org/9781108064590

© in this compilation Cambridge University Press 2013

This edition first published 1856
This digitally printed version 2013

ISBN 978-1-108-06459-0 Paperback

MEMOIRS

OF

MRS. FITZHERBERT.

MRS. FITZHERBERT.

London: Richard Bentley 1856.

MEMOIRS

OF

MRS. FITZHERBERT;

WITH AN

ACCOUNT OF HER MARRIAGE
WITH H.R.H. THE PRINCE OF WALES,
AFTERWARDS KING GEORGE THE FOURTH.

BY THE HON. CHARLES LANGDALE.

LONDON:
RICHARD BENTLEY, NEW BURLINGTON STREET,
Publisher in Ordinary to Her Majesty.
M.DCCC.LVI.

LONDON :

WOODFALL AND KINDER, PRINTERS,

ANGEL COURT, SKINNER STREET.

DEDICATION.

———◆———

MY DEAR LORD STOURTON,

You will recollect forwarding to me, on the death of your lamented Father, a sealed parcel of papers addressed to me, and to be delivered unopened.

I believe, also, that you were aware that these papers referred to the principal events connected with the Marriage of the late Mrs. Fitzherbert with the then Prince of Wales, afterwards George the Fourth. The superscription of this packet marked its confidential character, and I had fondly hoped, that, as I had received this deposit from the hands of your respected Parent to be used only in defence of the unblemished reputation of a dear friend and near relative, and of the religion which they in common professed, I might have transmitted it, under the same obligations, and under the same reservations, to one who might be willing to accept the trust, when I could no longer fulfil its conditions. Unhappily I am no longer

in a position to delegate to another a charge which I
had voluntarily taken upon myself. It is now more
than a twelvemonth since my attention was called
to a gross attack upon the honour and virtue of Mrs.
Fitzherbert. As this charge, if substantiated, would
equally damage the religion which sanctioned her union
with the Prince of Wales, and her own conduct under
such sanction, I feel myself bound to fulfil the pledge
given to my Brother, your revered Father; and to em-
ploy all the means placed at my disposal to rescue
both a Catholic lady and the Catholic Church from the
opprobrium which would attach to them, if the aspersions contained in the " Memoirs of the Whig Party,"
by the late Lord Holland, and edited by his Son, were
founded on facts.

You will find in these pages the copy of a note
written by your Father, which appeared at the end of
the *Edinburgh Review*, No. 136, soon after the death
of Mrs. Fitzherbert, in 1837, in consequence of some
observations made in a former number of that Review.
Notwithstanding this, Lord Holland assumes the truth
of his anecdote, upon the very ground upon which your
Father's authorised statement of the doctrine of the
Catholic Church would prove its falsity. Any attempt,
therefore, by such limited means of contradiction would

appear to have been wholly ineffectual for placing in its true light that portion of the history of the Life of George the Fourth which may be connected with his Marriage with Mrs. Fitzherbert. As the character of the latter must depend upon this Marriage being seen in its true light, as far as she was morally and conscientiously a party to it, I have therefore determined to lay every circumstance connected with it fully and fairly before the public.

As this course is the one which I believe will most effectually carry out the primary object of my late Brother, your excellent Father, and is founded in a great degree on his honourable testimony, I think I cannot adopt a better course to redeem a pledge given to the Father, than to dedicate these pages to his worthy Son.

Believe me,

Your affectionate Uncle,

CHARLES LANGDALE.

Houghton, Dec. 22, 1855.

THE RIGHT HON. LORD STOURTON.

MEMOIRS

OF

MRS. FITZHERBERT.

THE subject of the present Memoir, Mary Anne
Smythe, was daughter of Walter Smythe, Esq., of
Brambridge, in the county of Hants, second son of
Sir John Smythe, Baronet, of Eske, in the county
of Durham, and Acton Burnell, in Shropshire. She
was born in July, 1756, and married, in July, 1775,
Edward Weld, Esq., of Lulworth Castle, in the county
of Dorset, who died in the course of the same year.
She married, secondly, Thomas Fitzherbert, Esq., of
Swinnerton, in the county of Stafford, in the year
1778.   He only survived their union three years,
leaving her a second time a widow, before she had
attained the age of twenty-five.

It was about four years after the death of Mr.
Fitzherbert that she first became acquainted with the

youthful heir to the Throne of Great Britain, who was then about twenty-three years of age, and the most accomplished Prince of Europe. The events to which this acquaintance gave rise will form the matter of the following pages. It will be my endeavour to limit my observations to these circumstances, and carefully to avoid those political questions, interesting as they might have been to the historian, but foreign to the object as to the motives which have induced me to undertake the more limited view of the part which Mrs. Fitzherbert had in the history of that day.

At the close of the last year* my attention was first drawn, by an article in the *Dublin Review*, " On the Memoirs of the Whig Party, by the late Lord Holland, edited by his son, Henry Edward Lord Holland," to certain calumnious charges, advanced by Lord Holland, on the authority of some unnamed individual, but asserted by his Lordship to be " a man of strict veracity," against the fair character and honest prin-

---

* It was hoped that these pages, which were considerably advanced, might have appeared before the close of the year 1855. It has not been thought necessary to alter the reference to the supposed period of publication, as the dates of the correspondence will sufficiently point out to the reader the times and circumstances to which they allude.

ciples of Mrs. Fitzherbert, in relation to her connection with George the Fourth, then Prince of Wales.

The more important circumstances attendant upon the relationship established between this Lady and the then Prince of Wales have now become matter of history. Willingly would I have left the more private details of the formation of this connection in the obscurity best befitting the delicacy of a lady's life, had not the reproach of a dishonest connection and abandoned principle arisen out of the account which the late Lord Holland has stated on the authority of an unnamed informant, and which his son has thought himself justified in publishing to the world.

The charge, and the grounds of it, are thus brought forward by Lord Holland, in his "Memoirs of the Whig Party:"*—

"The exact date and circumstances of that ceremony" (alluding to the Marriage, which his Lordship admits to have taken place,) "have not come to my knowledge; but the account given of some part of the transaction by Mrs. Fitzherbert herself to a friend of mine, a man of strict veracity, is curious, and, I believe, correct. 'It was at the

* Vol. II. p. 140.

Prince's own earnest and repeated solicitations—not at Mrs. Fitzherbert's request, that any ceremony was resorted to.'

" She knew it to be invalid in law : she thought it nonsense, and told the Prince so. In proof that such had been her uniform opinion, she adduced a very striking circumstance — namely, that no ceremony by a Roman Catholic priest took place at all ; the most obvious method of allaying her scruples, had she had any. I believe, therefore, that she spoke with truth when she frankly owned ' that she had given herself up to him, exacted no conditions, trusted to his honour, and set no value on the ceremony which he insisted on having solemnised.' It was performed by an English clergyman. A certificate was signed by him, and attested by two witnesses, both, I believe, Catholic gentlemen, and one a near relation of Mrs. Fitzherbert—Mr. Errington. Mrs. Fitzherbert, from mixed feelings of fear and generosity, tore off the names of the witnesses at some subsequent period, lest they should by possibility be involved in any legal penalties for being present at an illegal transaction. Before George the Fourth's accession to the throne, or, as I believe, his appointment to the Regency, the clergyman was dead (for it was not, as often surmised,

Parson Johnes who married them); and his name, I understand, remains annexed to the instrument purporting to be a register or certificate of the ceremony.

If any corroboration were necessary to substantiate facts, of which such proofs are extant, and to which there are so many unexceptionable testimonies, it would be found in the behaviour of Mrs. Fitzherbert on many subsequent occasions, and in the uniform respect and attention which she has received from nearly all the branches of the Royal Family."

Lord Holland, elsewhere in his Memoirs, had already referred to the proofs that the Marriage ceremony had taken place between the Prince and Mrs. Fitzherbert, and even that the former had, at his subsequent Marriage with the Princess of Brunswick, quailed under its recollection. The Memoirs* say:—" This manifest repugnance to the Marriage was attributed by many, at the time, to remorse at the recollection of a similar ceremony which had passed between him and Mrs. Fitzherbert. The subsequent conduct of all the parties, and the treatment of Mrs. Fitzherbert by all branches of the Royal Family, even when separated from the Prince, have long since confirmed the suspicion. In truth, that there was such a ceremony, is

* Vol. II. p. 153.

now (I transcribe my narrative in 1836) not matter of conjecture or inference, but of history. Documents proving it, long in the possession of Mrs. Fitzherbert's family, have been since June, 1833, actually deposited by agreement between the executors of George the Fourth (the Duke of Wellington and Sir William Knighton), and the nominees of Mrs. Fitzherbert (Lord Albemarle and Lord Stourton), at Coutts's Bank, in a sealed box, bearing a superscription of, ' The property of the Earl of Albemarle; but not to be opened by him without apprising the Duke of Wellington, or words to that purport."

Still, in the face of these facts, Lord Holland gives credence, and his son circulation, to the insulting imputation conveyed by his friend, " a man of strict veracity," that Mrs. Fitzherbert had no scruples—that she had given herself up to him—exacted no conditions, and set no value on the ceremony, which " he (the Prince, forsooth!) insisted upon being solemnised," and not Mrs. Fitzherbert.

In reciting such sentiments, and in adopting them, Lord Holland does but too apparently sanction the easy morality of his relative, Mr. Fox, quoted by him in relation to this subject and to this lady. Mr. Fox's letter to the Prince of Wales, on the subject of

the Marriage between him and Mrs. Fitzherbert I
here subjoin, as well as the Prince's reply:—

"December 10, 1785.

" SIR,

" I hope your Royal Highness does me the justice
to believe, that it is with the utmost reluctance I
trouble you with my opinion unasked at any time, much
more so upon a subject where it may not be agreeable
to your wishes. I am sure that nothing could ever
make me take this liberty, but the condescension which
you have honoured me with upon so many occasions,
and the zealous and grateful attachment that I feel for
your Royal Highness, and which makes me run the
risk even of displeasing you, for the purpose of doing
you a real service.

" I was told just before I left town yesterday, that
Mrs. Fitzherbert was arrived; and if I had heard only
this, I should have felt the most unfeigned joy at an
event which I knew would contribute so much to your
Royal Highness's satisfaction; but I was told at the
same time, that, from a variety of circumstances which
had been observed and put together, there was reason
to suppose that you were going to take the very desperate step (pardon the expression) of marrying her at this

moment.　If such an idea be really in your mind, and
it be not now too late, for God's sake let me call your
attention to some considerations which my attachment
to your Royal Highness, and the real concern which I
take in whatever relates to your interest, have suggested
to me, and which may possibly have the more weight
with you, when you perceive that Mrs. Fitzherbert is
equally interested in most of them with yourself.　In
the first place, you are aware that a Marriage with a
Catholic throws the Prince contracting such Marriage
out of the succession of the Crown.　Now, what change
may have happened in Mrs. Fitzherbert's sentiments
upon religious matters I know not; but I do not understand that any public profession of change has been
made.　Surely, Sir, this is not a matter to be trifled
with; and your Royal Highness must excuse the extreme freedom with which I write.　If there should be
a doubt about her previous conversion, consider the circumstances in which you stand.　The King not feeling
for you as a father ought; the Duke of York professedly
his favourite, and likely to be married agreeably to the
King's wishes; the nation full of its old prejudices
against Catholics, and justly dreading all disputes about
succession;—in all these circumstances your enemies
might take such advantage as I shudder to think of;

and though your generosity might think no sacrifice too great to be made to a person whom you love so entirely, consider what her reflections must be in such an event, and how impossible it would be for her ever to forgive herself.

"I have stated this danger upon the supposition that the Marriage would be a real one: but your Royal Highness knows as well as I, that according to the present laws of the country it *cannot;* and I need not point out to your good sense, what a source of uneasiness it must be to you, to her, and above all to the nation, to have it a matter of dispute and discussion, whether the Prince of Wales is or is not married. All speculations on the feelings of the public are uncertain; but I doubt much whether an uncertainty of this kind, by keeping men's minds in perpetual agitation upon a matter of this moment, might not cause a greater ferment than any other possible situation.

"If there should be children from the Marriage, I need not say how much the uneasiness as well of yourselves as of the nation must be aggravated. If anything could add to the weight of these considerations, it is the impossibility of remedying the mischiefs I have alluded to; for if your Royal Highness should think proper, when you are

twenty-five years old, to notify to Parliament your intention to marry (by which means *alone* a *legal* Marriage can be contracted), in what manner can it be
notified? If the previous Marriage is mentioned or
owned, will it not be said that you have set at defiance
the laws of your country; and that you now come to
Parliament for a sanction for what you have already
done in contempt of it? If there are children, will it
not be said that we must look for future applications
to legitimate them, and consequently be liable to disputes for the succession between the eldest son, and
the eldest son after the legal Marriage? And will not
the entire annulling the whole Marriage be suggested
as the most secure way of preventing all such disputes?

" If the Marriage is not mentioned to Parliament,
but yet is known to have been solemnized, as it certainly
will be known if it takes place, these are the consequences:—First, that at all events any child born in
the interim is immediately illegitimated; and next,
that arguments will be drawn from the circumstances
of the concealed Marriage against the public one. It
will be said, that a woman who has lived with you as
your wife without being so, is not fit to be Queen of
England; and thus the very thing that is done for the
sake of her reputation will be used against it: and

what would make this worse would be, the Marriage
being known (though not officially communicated to
Parliament), it would be impossible to deny the assertion; whereas, if there was no Marriage, I conclude
your intercourse would be carried on, as it ought, in so
private a way as to make it wholly inconsistent with
decency or propriety for any one in public to hazard
such a suggestion.

"If, in consequence of your notification, steps
should be taken in Parliament, and an Act be
passed (which, considering the present state of the
power of the King and Ministry, is more than probable)
to prevent your Marriage, you will be reduced to the
most difficult of all dilemmas with respect to the footing upon which your Marriage is to stand for the future;
and your children will be born to pretensions which
must make their situation unhappy, if not dangerous.
These situations appear to me of all others the most to
be pitied; and the more so, because the more indications persons born in such circumstances give of spirit,
talents, or anything that is good, the more will they be
suspected and oppressed, and the more will they regret
the being deprived of what they must naturally think
themselves entitled to.

"I could mention many other considerations upon
this business, if I did not think those I have stated

of so much importance, that smaller ones would divert your attention from them rather than add to their weight. That I have written with a freedom which on any other occasion would be unbecoming, I readily confess; and nothing would have induced me to do it, but a deep sense of my duty to a Prince who has honoured me with so much of his confidence, and who would have but an ill return for all his favours and goodness to me, if I were to avoid speaking truth to him, however disagreeable, at so critical a juncture. The sum of my humble advice, nay, of my most earnest entreaty, is this—that your Royal Highness would not think of marrying till you can marry legally. When that time comes, you must judge for yourself; and no doubt you will take into consideration, both what is due to private honour and your public station. In the meanwhile, a mock Marriage (for it can be no other) is neither honourable for any of the parties, nor, with respect to your Royal Highness, even safe. This appears so clear to me, that, if I were Mrs. Fitzherbert's father or brother, I would advise her not by any means to agree to it, and to prefer any other species of connection with you to one leading to so much misery and mischief.

" It is high time I should finish this very long and, perhaps your Royal Highness will think, ill-timed letter;

but such as it is, it is dictated by pure zeal and attachment to your Royal Highness. With respect to Mrs. Fitzherbert, she is a person with whom I have scarcely the honour of being acquainted, but I hear from everybody that her character is irreproachable and her manners most amiable. Your Royal Highness knows, too, that I have not in my mind the same objection to intermarriages with Princes and subjects which many have. But under the present circumstances a Marriage at present appears to me to be the most desperate measure for all parties concerned, that their worst enemies could have suggested."

The following was the reply of the Prince of Wales to Mr. Fox :—

"MY DEAR CHARLES,

" Your letter of last night afforded me more true satisfaction than I can find words to express; as it is an additional proof to me (which I assure you I did not want) of your having that true regard and affection for me, which it is not only the wish but the ambition of my life to merit. Make yourself easy, my dear friend. Believe me, the world will now soon be convinced, that there not only is, but never was, any grounds for these reports, which of late have been so malevolently circulated. I have not seen you since the apos-

tacy of Eden. I think it ought to have the same effect
upon all our friends that it has upon me—I mean the
linking us closer to each other; and I believe you will
easily believe these to be my sentiments; for you are
perfectly well acquainted with my ways of thinking
upon these sort of subjects. When I say my ways of
thinking, I think I had better say my old maxim, which
I ever intend to adhere to—I mean that of swimming
or sinking with my friends. I have not time to add
much more, except just to say, that I believe I shall
meet you at dinner at Bushey on Tuesday; and to desire you to believe me at all times, my dear Charles,
most affectionately yours,

                    (Signed)   " GEORGE P."
        " Carlton House,
    " Sunday morning, 2 o'clock,
        " December 11th, 1785."

Who and what is the woman whom this teacher
of morality would sacrifice at the shrine of princely
satisfaction and political expedience? Mr. Fox says,
" With respect to Mrs. Fitzherbert, she is a person
with whom I have scarcely the honour of being acquainted, but I hear from everybody that her *character
is irreproachable,* and her manners most amiable."
    Such is the letter, and such the mode of dealing

with a lady of irreproachable character, recommended therein to the then youthful Prince of Wales! Well, indeed, may princes be pitied, when the counsels of age, aided by the highest political position, only point out to the passions of youth, not how they are to be curbed, but how they may be gratified!

With such principles, the " veracity of a friend " may be easily understood, as disposing of all the dictates of religion, of all the most estimable virtues of a woman who was described to have " no scruples," provided appearances were preserved ; to be regardless of the distinction between the concubine and the wife of a Prince; and to be as ready to submit to the moral depravity of the one portion, as to insist on the honoured rights of the other.

However, that Mrs. Fitzherbert would not, did not, thus degrade herself, and violate all the principles of her religion, by yielding to the solicitations of the Prince, or to the counsels of his profligate advisers, and that, in spite of the " veracity " of Lord Holland's friend, this virtuous and high-principled lady did only consent to receive the Prince of Wales in the character of her husband, every public and private testimony, nay, even the details in the Memoirs themselves, to every well-constituted mind sufficiently attest.

These Memoirs state, that Mrs. Fitzherbert had left England and retired to the Continent, to escape from the importunity of the Prince. They detail the despair, almost amounting to madness, on the part of the Prince, at this step taken by a virtuous woman to avoid the attempts made upon her honour by a Prince, who had indeed but little experience of the power exercised by religion over the conduct of a Catholic lady. They prove, moreover, that her principles had taught her to resist all the fascinations of the most accomplished gentleman, united, in her devoted admirer, to the highest princely rank.

Lord Holland says, that " Mrs. Fox, then Mrs. Armistead, had repeatedly assured him, that the Prince came down more than once to converse with her and Mr. Fox on the subject; that he cried by the hour; that he testified the sincerity and violence of his passion and despair by extravagant expressions and actions —rolling on the floor, striking his forehead, tearing his hair, falling into hysterics, and swearing that he would abandon the country, forego the Crown, &c."

What, then, were the inducements held out to Mrs. Fitzherbert, which brought her back to England? What, but an offer of Marriage made by the Prince,

in spite of the earnest remonstrances of his friend and
adviser, Mr. Fox, already alluded to?

Yet, in spite of all these remonstrances, Lord
Holland would have us believe, that this heir to the
Throne was himself the originator, the promoter, nay,
the repeated and earnest solicitor for the performance
of a ceremony, the consequence of which might be so
fatal to his future rights. Yes; for "a veracious friend"
has assured Lord Holland that Mrs. Fitzherbert, for
fear any person should suspect her of being a virtuous,
honest woman, was herself at the pains to convince this
truthful gentleman that she really thought such a Marriage ceremony "nonsense," and frankly owned herself
—what? anything but his wife?—a violator of the
laws of God, lost to the principles of her religion,
the degraded mistress, degraded to the rank of but
too many who have—as she is said to report of
herself—trusted to this honour, where their own
honour could only be contaminated by the contact!

In the face of all this, Lord Holland believes the
statement of the man of "*strict veracity*" to be correct; nay, though even he himself bears testimony to
the "uniform respect and attention which Mrs. Fitzherbert has received from nearly all branches of the
Royal Family"—yes, whilst she was at pains to prove

herself, in her own opinion at least, a worthless character, unfit for social intercourse with the chaste and
virtuous of her sex !

What more Lord Holland means by saying, that
"if any corroboration were necessary to substantiate
facts, of which such proofs are extant" (the Marriage),
" and to which there are so many unexceptionable
testimonies, it would be found in the behaviour of
Mrs. Fitzherbert on many subsequent occasions," I am
at a loss to imagine ; unless, to the charge of incon-
tinence, as advanced on the authority of his friend, his
Lordship himself wishes to add that of hypocrisy.

It is, however, known that Mr. Fox denied in
his place in Parliament that any ceremony of Marriage had taken place between the Prince of Wales
and Mrs. Fitzherbert.*   Whether Mr. Fox had, or had

---

* The following is given in " Croly's Life and Times of
George the Fourth," as Mr. Fox's reply to observations made by
Mr. Rolle. Such a denial can admit but of one construction, but
on whom rests its fabrication I am not disposed to observe.

" As to the allusions of the honourable member for Devon
(Rolle), of danger and so forth to the Church and State, I am not
bound to understand them, until he shall make them intelligible ;
but I suppose they are meant in reference to that *falsehood* which
has been so *scandalously* propagated out of doors, for the wanton
sport of the vulgar, and which I now pronounce, by *whomsoever*

not, the authority of the Prince for this denial, it is not now my business to inquire. Suffice it to say, that Mrs. Fitzherbert, in the Memoirs, is justly asserted not

invented, to be a miserable calumny, a low, malicious falsehood!" He had hoped, that in that House a tale, only fit to impose upon the lowest persons in the streets, would not have gained credit; but, when it appeared that an *invention* so monstrous, a report of what had not the smallest degree of foundation, had been circulated with so much industry as to make an impression on the mind of members of that House, it proved the extraordinary efforts made by the enemies of His Royal Highness to propagate the grossest and most malignant falsehoods, with a view to depreciate his character, and injure him in the opinion of the country. He was at a loss to imagine what *species* of party could have fabricated so base a calumny. Had there existed in the kingdom such a faction as an anti-Brunswick faction, to it he certainly should have imputed the invention of so malicious a falsehood; for he knew not what other description of men could have felt an interest in first forming, and then circulating, with more than ordinary assiduity, a tale in every particular so unfounded. His Royal Highness had authorised him to declare, that, as a Peer of Parliament, he was ready, in the other House, to submit to any the most pointed questions; or to afford His Majesty, or His Majesty's Ministers, the fullest assurances of the utter falsehood of the statement in question, which never had, and which common sense must see never could have, happened.

"In reply to Mr. Rolle, whether what Mr. Fox had said was to be understood as spoken from direct authority, Mr. Fox replied, 'that he had direct authority.'"—*Annual Register*, 1787.

to have disguised her resentment. "She would not speak to Mr. Fox. There can be little doubt that she urged the Prince to take some step to procure a public disavowal of a declaration which he knew to be false." Indeed, the Memoirs go on to state, that, the morning after Mr. Fox's statement, "the Prince sent for Mr. Grey (Lord Howick and Earl Grey), who was then in high favour with him, and after much preamble, and pacing in a hurried manner about the room, exclaimed, 'Charles' (he always so called Mr. Fox) 'certainly went too far last night. You, my dear Grey, shall explain it;' and then in distinct terms (as Grey has *since the Prince's death* assured me), though with prodigious agitation, owned that a ceremony *had* taken place. Mr. Grey observed, 'that Mr. Fox must unquestionably suppose, that he had authority for all he said, and that, if there had been any mistake, it could only be rectified by His Royal Highness speaking to Mr. Fox himself, and setting him right on such matters as had been misunderstood between them: no other person can,' he added, 'be employed, without questioning Mr. Fox's veracity, which nobody, I presume, is prepared to do.'

　"This answer *chagrined, disappointed, and agitated Prince exceedingly; and after some exclamations* of annoyance, he threw himself on a sofa, muttering, 'Well, then, Sheridan must say something.'"*

The effort made by the Prince to persuade Mrs. Fitzherbert that he was not a party to Mr. Fox's denial of the Marriage between them, is curiously illustrated by the following anecdote, which I have on the authority of Mr. Bodenham, the brother-in-law of Lord Stourton, who received this account from Lord Stourton:—Mrs. Fitzherbert was on a visit with the Honourable Mrs. Butler, her friend and relative, and at whose house the Prince frequently met Mrs. Fitzherbert. The Prince called the morning after the denial of the Marriage in the House of Commons by Mr. Fox. He went up to Mrs. Fitzherbert, and taking hold of both

* Croly again reports as the reply of Mr. Sheridan, in allusion to Mr. Fox's offer on the part of the Prince of Wales to undergo an examination in the House of Lords, "that the House deserved credit for decorum, in not taking advantage of the offer, and demanding such an inquiry. But while His Royal Highness's feelings had been, doubtless, considered on the occasion, he must take the liberty of saying, however some might think it a subordinate consideration, that there was another person, entitled, in every honourable and delicate mind, to the same attention; one whom he would not otherwise venture to describe, or allude to, but by saying it was a name which malice or ignorance alone could attempt to injure, and whose character and conduct claimed and were entitled to the truest respect."

her hands and caressing her, said, "Only conceive,
Maria, what Fox did yesterday. He went down to the
House and denied that you and I were man and wife!
Did you ever hear of such a thing?" Mrs. Fitzher-
bert made no reply, but changed countenance and
turned pale.

Now, how again is all this consistent with Lord
Holland's story and charge against Mrs. Fitzherbert?
How could she be indignant at the denial of a ceremony having taken place, which she herself had "*told
the Prince was all nonsense?*" Who then, and what,
forced the Prince to send for Mr. Grey? What occasioned his agitated conduct, the struggle with which
he at last owned to him that a ceremony had taken
place, and his resolve to call upon Mr. Sheridan to
make an explanation or disavowal, which he would
not, according to Mr. Grey's suggestion, claim from
Mr. Fox himself? Was all this awkward dilemma,
in the opinion of Lord Holland, owing to a virtuous
scruple on the part of the Prince to correct a misapprehension of his friend Charles (as he called him), or
was it to the outraged honour of an "irreproachable
woman," unwilling to consent to be classed amongst
those of her sex who are ready to disregard the sacred
rites of the Marriage contract; a woman who insisted

upon the reparation due to her wounded reputation, by a disavowal as publicly made, and in the same House of Parliament which had heard the stigma cast upon her?

But, according to Lord Holland, a simple statement that she was not in her own opinion a wife, was not enough to satisfy Mrs. Fitzherbert; she would also proceed to prove it. " She adduced a very striking circumstance, namely, that no ceremony by a Catholic priest took place at all; the most obvious method of allaying her scruples, had she had any." No scruple about what? About living with a man who was not her husband?

Mrs. Fitzherbert was a Catholic, and educated in the principles of the Catholic religion, whose doctrine could admit no distinction between a prince and a peasant, condemning alike the criminal indulgences of either, and maintaining in both the indissoluble sacredness of the Marriage contract. But what does this additional proof of no Catholic priest, and therefore no Marriage, amount to? Why, to just as much as the whole story of the asseverations of Lord Holland's " man of strict veracity." In this case, as in every other, every circumstance proves the exact reverse of his statements, and of Lord Holland's deductions therefrom. The pre-

sence of a Catholic priest would not, in any way, have
added to the validity of the marriage in the eyes of
the Catholic Church; and, therefore, it is fair to conclude, would not have added to them in those of
Mrs. Fitzherbert, a well-educated Catholic, especially
likely to be well informed on the mode of conducting
the Marriage ceremony so as to fulfil the forms and
conditions required by her own Church, returning as
she was from the Catholic Continent with the special
intention of fulfilling those conditions, the absence of
which had driven her abroad.

What these conditions are required to be, are stated
in an article in the *Dublin Review*, commenting on the
very matter which forms the subject of these pages.
This article is understood to have been written by an
eminent theologian of the Irish Catholic Church.*

" The doctrine of the Catholic Church regarding
Marriage is plain and simple. She teaches that the
Marriage contract itself, which is perfected by the
words, ' I take thee for my wife,' on the part of the
man, and ' I take thee for my husband,' on the part of
the woman, or by any other words or signs by which
the contracting parties manifest their intention of
taking each other for man and wife, is a sacrament.

* Oct. 1854.

" Protestants are apt to fall into the mistake, that it is the priest who administers the sacrament to the wedded pair. He does no such thing. As far as the validity of the contract and of the sacrament is concerned, even when the contracting parties are both Catholics, the priest need not utter a word. His presence is only necessary as a *witness* to the contract between the parties.

" Up to the time of the Council of Trent, the presence of a priest was not necessary for the validity of either the contract or the sacrament; nor was it by any means to confer the sacrament that the Council enacted a law requiring his presence. The law was made in consequence of the abuses which arose from clandestine marriages ; because an immoral person, who had married without witnesses, could afterwards deny the existence of the contract, and wed another publicly, and in the face of the Church. To prevent this abuse, the Council of Trent enacted that the parish priest of one of the contracting parties, or some other priest deputed by him, and two other witnesses, should, for the future (*in posterum*) be present (*præsente parocho*) at the Marriage contract. The presence of the two other witnesses is required exactly in the same way as that of the parish priest. The law is simply that Marriage should be contracted in the presence of three witnesses, one of whom should necessarily be the parish priest. Nor was this law made at once obligatory even on Catholics. By an ordinance of the Council, it was not to have effect in *any parish* until thirty days after it had been published there. This allowed a large discretion to each bishop, with regard to the time of its publication in his diocese, and, in fact, it is not long since it has been introduced into England. But it does not, and never did, apply to any Marriage in those countries where one of the parties is not a Catholic. Neither in such marriages which are called mixed, nor in those contracted between parties neither of which belong to the Catholic Church, is the presence of any priest required for the validity of either the contract or the sacrament. It is not even necessary that the contracting parties should *know* that Marriage is a sacrament. The sacrament exists wherever Christians marry as Christ intended; and if they be properly disposed, they will receive grace to live happily together, and to bring up their children in the fear and love of God.

"Mrs. Fitzherbert's Marriage was, therefore, perfectly valid, both as a contract and as a sacrament, in the eyes of the whole Catholic Church; and to imagine that she alone, of all those who professed the same faith, should look upon it as invalid, is monstrously absurd. Neither the Pope nor the whole Church could have annulled it, nor allowed her to marry another.

"But it was illegal! Why, so was the whole Catholic religion at the same period. It was, not very long ago, unlawful to celebrate Mass—but the sacrifice was not therefore invalidly offered. To say that Mrs. Fitzherbert considered the Marriage ceremony to be 'nonsense' because it was illegal, at a time when the penal code against Catholics—and especially that part of it which regarded Matrimony—was in full operation, is about as reasonable as to prove, that she did not believe in Transubstantiation, because the law declared it to be damnable and idolatrous."

I am not, therefore, discussing the legality of the Marriage in the eye of English law. It is only within a few years, that a Marriage in England would be legal even between two Catholics, unless they consented to the insulting condition of appearing in a Protestant Church, and submitting to the ceremony to be there performed by a Protestant clergyman. What the Prince of Wales might have thought of this Marriage I am not called upon to say or prove; but without adopting either the supposition of Lord Holland or his friend, that it was "at *his* repeated and earnest solicitation the ceremony was resorted to," I can imagine no interpretation but one, by an upright and honourable mind, of a solemn pledge, whether, according to the form of law or not, to take a woman for his wife. Certainly this ceremony having been gone through before a clergyman of the Established Church might naturally have been supposed by Mrs. Fitzherbert to add to its authenticity, if not its legality, in the eyes of those, whether the Prince himself, his family, or the country, who professed the same religion. To herself, as a witness to the Marriage, and as such signing the certificate, it was equally obligatory, as if performed in the presence of a Catholic priest.

Such is the line of reasoning which I think must occur to every candid mind, on weighing, with fair consideration, a direct charge of criminal conduct against a Lady whose public character was admitted to be irreproachable, and towards whom the Royal Family of England testified uniform respect. It remains, that I should now proceed to show what special cause there is for publishing these pages, and why I now feel myself especially called upon, not only to direct the attention of the public to what I consider to be the natural deduction to be drawn from the charge itself as narrated by the author of the Memoirs, but to bring forward private details, which I would infinitely rather have left to the secret keeping wherein they were deposited by this virtuous lady. But I cannot forget that they were so left by her in trust for the sole defence of that character, which, instead of being herself the first to vilify (as asserted by Lord Holland,) all who knew her were well aware she was anxiously sensitive to defend from reproach.

It will have appeared, by an extract already given, from the Memoirs of Lord Holland, that my Brother, Lord Stourton, was one of the nominees with the Earl of Albemarle, to whose charge were committed certain documents, deposited by agreement with the executors of George the Fourth (the Duke of Wellington and Sir William Knighton), at Coutts's Bank, in a sealed box. It will hence not unnaturally be credited, that the late Lord Stourton was an intimate friend of Mrs. Fitzherbert. If I add to this, that there existed near relationship in blood, and the profession of the same religion, it may also account for those confidential communications which will form the substance of the following pages, and for that pledge which Mrs. Fitzherbert required, and received, from Lord Stourton, to defend her character from any

calumnious charges which might, in after time, be
brought against it.

A letter to Lord Stourton from Mrs. Fitzherbert,
dated Paris, Dec. 7, 1833, sufficiently expresses the
wishes and confidence of the writer:—" I trust, whenever it pleases God to remove me from this world,
that my conduct and character in your hands will not
disgrace my family and my friends."

It was not long before Lord Stourton felt himself
called upon to act upon the trust which had thus been
reposed in him.

In the very year following Mrs. Fitzherbert's death
the following observations appeared in the *Edinburgh
Review* :—

" The most excusable by far, indeed the most respectable, of all the Prince's attachments, had been that
which he had early formed for Mrs. Fitzherbert, a woman of the most amiable qualities, and the most exem-
plary virtue.   Her abilities were not shining, nor were
her personal charms dazzling, nor was she even in the
first stage of youth ; but her talents were of the most
engaging kind ; she had a peculiarly sweet disposition,
united to sterling good sense, and was possessed of
manners singularly fascinating.   His passion for this
excellent person was a redeeming virtue of the Prince ;
it could only proceed from a fund of natural sense and

good taste, which, had it but been managed with ordinary prudence and care, would have endowed a most distinguished character in private life; and could it by any miracle have been well managed in a palace, must have furnished out a ruler before whose lustre the fame of Titus and the Antonines would grow pale. This passion was heightened by the difficulties which its virtuous object interposed to its gratification; and upon no other terms than Marriage could that be obtained.

"But Marriage with this admirable lady was forbidden by law! She was a Roman Catholic. Sincerely attached to the religion of her forefathers, she refused to purchase a crown by conforming to any other; and the law declared, that whoever married a Catholic should forfeit all right to the crown of these realms, as if he were naturally dead. This law, however, was unknown to her, and, blinded by various pretences, she was induced to consent to a clandestine Marriage, which is supposed to have been solemnized between her and the Prince beyond the limits of the English dominions; in the silly belief, perhaps, entertained by him, that he escaped the penalty to which his reckless conduct exposed him, and that the forfeiture of his succession to the crown was only denounced against such a Marriage if contracted within the realm.

" The consent of the Sovereign was another requisite
of the law to render the Marriage valid: that consent
had not been obtained; and the invalidity of the contract was supposed to save the forfeiture. But they
who so construed the plain provision in the Bill of
Rights, assumed, first, that no forfeiture could be incurred by doing an act which was void in itself, whereas
the law of England, as well as of Scotland, and every
other country, abounds in cases of acts prohibited and
made void, yet punished by a forfeiture of the rights
of him who contravenes the prohibition, as much as if
they were valid and effectual.

" The same courtly reasoners and fraudulent match-
makers of Carlton House next assumed, that statutes
so solemn as the Bill of Rights and Act of Settlement
could be varied, and, indeed, repealed in an essential
particular, most clearly within their mischief, by a subsequent law which makes not the least reference whatever to their provisions; while no man could doubt,
that to prevent even the attempt at contravening those
prohibitions was the object of the acts, in order to prevent all risks; it being equally manifest, that if merely
preventing a Catholic from being the Sovereign's consort had been the only purpose of the enactment, this
could have been most effectually accomplished by simply

declaring the Marriage void, and the forfeiture of the crown became wholly superfluous.

" It is, therefore, very far from being clear, that this Marriage was no forfeiture of the crown. But, it may be said, the Prince ran this risk only for himself, and no one has a right to complain. Not so. The forfeiture of the crown was his own risk assuredly; but he trepanned Mrs. Fitzherbert into a sacrifice of her honour to gratify his passion, when he well knew, that the ceremony which she was made to believe a Marriage, could only be regarded as a mere empty form, of no legal validity or effect whatever; unless, indeed, that of exposing her and all who assisted, to the high pains and penalties of a *premunire*. While he pretended that he was making her his wife, and made her believe she was such, he was only making her the victim of his passions, and the accomplice of his crimes.

" A few years after, when those passions had cooled, or were directed into some new channel, the rumour having got abroad, a question was asked in Parliament respecting the alleged Marriage. His chosen political associates were appealed to, and, being instructed by him, denied the charge in the most unqualified terms. Before such men as Mr. Fox and Mr. Grey could thus far commit their honour, they took care

to be well assured of the fact, by direct personal communication with the Prince himself. He most solemnly
denied the whole upon his sacred honour; and his denial was, through these most respectable channels, conveyed to the House of Commons. We are giving here
a matter of history well known at the time;—a thousand times repeated since, and never qualified by the
parties, or contradicted on their behalf." *

This charge against the conduct and character of
Mrs. Fitzherbert brought out from Lord Stourton the
following note, which appeared at the end of the succeeding number of this Review :†—

" Note to the article on George the Fourth and
Queen Caroline in Number 135.

" We have received from Lord Stourton a letter
respecting our notice in the above article of Mrs.
Fitzherbert's Marriage; and we have much pleasure
in laying before our readers a communication so
creditable to the feelings of the noble writer.

"To the Editor of the Edinburgh Review.
" Sir,

"A misstatement, no doubt unintentional, of the
circumstances attending the Marriage of Mrs. Fitzher-

* Edinburgh Review, No. cxxxv.   † No. cxxxvi.

bert, in one of your late articles, being liable to a construction, in the views of members of her religious
communion, injurious to her reputation, you will, I am
sure, readily oblige me by inserting in your next Number the following more accurate statement, for the
fidelity of which I pledge my honour.

"The Marriage ceremony was performed, *not out of
this kingdom*, as you have stated, but in her own
drawing-room, in her house in town, in the presence of
an officiating Protestant clergyman, and of two of her
own nearest relatives. All the parties being now
deceased, to ordinary readers this discrepancy will appear of little moment; as the ceremony, wherever it
was performed, could confer no legal rights; and no
issue followed this union. But when I inform you,
that, in the one case—that stated in your article—it
would have been an invalid Marriage as affecting the
conscience of Mrs. Fitzherbert in the sight of her own
Church; and that, in the other case, it formed a conscientious connection in the opinion of such portions
of Christendom as hold communion with the See of
Rome, I am confident you will permit this statement,
under my name and responsibility, to appear in your
Journal. I shall, moreover, add, that the conscientious validity of the contract depended upon the fact,

that the discipline of the Council of Trent as to Marriage has never been received in this country.

" I owe this plain counter-statement to the memory of Mrs. Fitzherbert, in order that aspersions, which, from peculiar circumstances, she was herself unable to rebut when living, should not be inscribed without contradiction on her tomb. That I have not officiously imposed on myself an unnecessary duty, in endeavouring to protect the fame of this virtuous and distinguished Lady, or am about to mislead by erroneous facts, I must appeal to the following extract from one of Mrs. Fitzherbert's letters to myself, which closely followed certain confidential communications, on which I rely for the perfect accuracy of my information on this delicate subject.

" ' MY DEAR LORD STOURTON,

" ' I trust whenever it pleases God to remove me from this world, that my conduct and character, in your hands, will not disgrace my family or my friends, Paris, Dec. 7, 1833.'

" I remain, Sir,

" Your obedient humble servant,

" STOURTON."

" Mansfield Street, 30th June, 1838."

I need hardly say how ineffective this note and explanation have proved, to screen the character of Mrs. Fitzherbert from obloquy, when Lord Holland's son allows his father's Memoirs to charge the very circumstance here brought forward by Lord Stourton in defence of the conscientious connection of Mrs. Fitzherbert with the Prince of Wales in the opinion of Catholic Christendom, as a proof that she had no scruple of "giving herself up and exacting no conditions," &c.

If proof were wanting of how little avail notices of this description are usually found to be, in arresting the course of calumnious censure on the memories of the dead, the explanation of Lord Stourton on this Marriage ceremony in a public Review in 1838, might, indeed, be placed in juxtaposition with these Memoirs, edited in 1854.

I am bound, however, to admit, that contradictions of this description are seldom read, and if read are seldom remembered; and that in this case the noble editor of his Father's Memoirs had probably never either seen or heard of the note by Lord Stourton in the *Edinburgh Review*. Indeed, much further than this, a very able commentary in the *Dublin Review*, on the very charges brought by Lord Holland against Mrs. Fitzherbert (to which allusion has already been made,

and an extract from it introduced), has proved wholly
ineffectual in preventing the propagation of the very
same charges; for the story in "the Memoirs" has
evidently been copied in a publication issued from the
press during the course of the present year.

I have stated the confidential trust reposed in my
brother, Lord Stourton, by Mrs. Fitzherbert, and have
quoted the very words in which she confides "her
conduct and character to his hands." In the year
1842, my brother made me acquainted with the
position in which he felt himself placed with regard
to the memory of this distinguished Lady and very
amiable relative, who was then dead. In the declining
state of his health at that time he expressed a not un-
natural anxiety, to deposit in other hands those confidential communications which he had received from
Mrs. Fitzherbert, together with the trust which he
had accepted, to avail himself of them for the defence
of her honour and reputation, should they be from
any quarter assailed. On placing certain manuscripts
in my hands which contained such particulars as he
had thought it desirable to commit to paper, he expressed his wish, that I should peruse them, and with
them receive that trust which had been reposed in
him by Mrs. Fitzherbert. The fulfilment of the con-

ditions of this trust, after his death, he wished to delegate to me; and in accordance with these views I received from my brother the following letter:—

"DEAR LANGDALE,

" With your kind permission I have confided all the papers relating to Mrs. Fitzherbert to your discretion and entire control, as I am competent to do so. The narrative you will find amongst them, however, prepared for publication, is merely to place before you, or any others whom you are or may be desirous of perusing it, a short biographical account of the leading incidents in the life of this distinguished and amiable personage, without more publicity than you may deem essential to the protection of her innocence, or for the maintenance of the character of her Church, which, upon being directly applied to, had at Rome sanctioned her connection with the Prince, and is, therefore, amenable to the same tribunal of public opinion as herself.

" This twofold interest of justice towards an irreproachable individual, and justice to her religion, which is bound up with this guardianship of the documents committed to my care, renders me anxious, when I can no more protect them myself,

to confide them to hands where, as in your own, I
feel a full confidence that they will be preserved and
disposed of with all discretion towards the public, and
regard for the interests of religion and of the character
of Mrs. Fitzherbert, should it be assailed by future
writers, supported as their testimonies may be by
false or spurious records, impeaching the virtue of
the deceased Lady, or of the authorities which up-
held and approved her conduct.

" Believe me,

" My dear Charles,

" Your affectionate Brother,

" STOURTON."

"Dec. 22, 1842.
" HON. CHARLES LANGDALE."

This letter will sufficiently show the importance
attached by my brother to the trust reposed in him by
Mrs. Fitzherbert, and especially to the connection
between the recognition of the conscientious character
of her Marriage with the Prince of Wales and the
Church to which Mrs. Fitzherbert and he equally be-
longed.   As this latter ground is advanced by Lord
Stourton in a communication with Lord Albemarle as
forming a peculiar responsibility on his own part, as

nember of the Catholic Church, and in this respect imposing an additional obligation on him, to which Lord Albemarle was not subject, I think it will be desirable to give the substance of a letter addressed by the former to his co-trustee; especially as therein are shown the reasons which influenced him in addressing the *Edinburgh Review.*

"10, Mansfield Street.

"MY DEAR LORD,

"Your Lordship will, perhaps, see in the public papers a paragraph with my name attached to it, and written by myself, of which your Lordship may possibly disapprove. I have thought much upon the delicacy of the trust out of which this paragraph has arisen, and the peculiar responsibility of my own situation (in part only shared by your Lordship), being the guardian alike of the unsullied reputation of Mrs. Fitzherbert, conscientiously connected with George the Fourth in Marriage, and of the character of my own Church, which has sanctioned the contract. Had there existed an entire community between us of duties in this to me arduous and delicate trust, I should have felt strongly, I am sure, disposed to be guided by your Lordship's counsels. But knowing that this cannot be the case, I

E

determined, after some months' deliberation, dating from
the perusal of the article in the *Edinburgh Review*,
imputing to Mrs. Fitzherbert, being ' an accomplice in
crimes,' to make myself individually and singly re-
sponsible for an explanation, without taking counsel of
any person whatever to share my responsibilities, and
the hazards that may follow such a course as I have
adopted.   But with Parliamentary history, and now
our most influential periodical history, against her, I
determined to give a true statement to the public, and
without allusion to any documents, to pledge at least
my own personal character to an attestation of the
truth, and of the purity of her fame.   And I will not
deny to your Lordship that I selected the time, as the
best fitted to give a public denial, in the face of
Christendom, to the many imputations she had to bear
when living, but which ought not to be engraven on
her tomb.

" In your Lordship, I am sure, I shall have a favourable interpreter of my motives, even were you con-
strained to condemn the prudence of the act.   I have
written this note simultaneously with the insertion of
the paragraph in the newspaper, that your Lordship
should not see that paragraph without hearing from
myself the cause assigned for its publication, and my

reasons for my not previously applying to your Lordship for advice on the occasion.

"I beg your Lordship to make any use of this letter that your Lordship may deem expedient or satisfactory to yourself.

"I beg to remain,

"With my sincere respects,

"Your Lordship's faithful

"and obliged servant,

"STOURTON."

"To THE EARL OF ALBEMARLE,

&c., &c."

The double responsibility, alluded to by Lord Stourton in the above letter, is of course shared by myself in accepting the trust which my brother delegated to me. The union of these two duties, the defence of the character of Mrs. Fitzherbert, and the connection of her Marriage with the principles of our common Church, cannot be better exemplified than by the very terms of the charge brought against her, in that it makes the supposed rules of the Church the ground of an accusation of unscrupulous profligacy, at the very time that she was adhering to its injunctions, and, as will appear, receiving a solemn sanction for her Marriage.

The death of my brother, Lord Stourton, on the 4th of December, 1846, called upon me to come to some resolution as to the course I ought to pursue in consequence of having accepted these delegated trusts. From his executor, the present Lord Stourton, I received a parcel of papers sealed, with the superscription in the handwriting of the late Lord, " To be delivered, unopened, to the Hon. Charles Langdale." One of the first of these papers referred to the documents now publicly known to be deposited in the bank of Messrs. Coutts.   It was as follows :—

" These papers are placed by Mrs. Fitzherbert at Messrs. Coutts and Co., at the disposal of the Earl of Albemarle and Lord Stourton, according to a memorandum dated the 24th August, 1833.

(Signed)   " WELLINGTON.

" ALBEMARLE.

" STOURTON."

" The above is a true Copy of the endorsement on a sealed packet left in the care of Messrs. Coutts and Co. by the Earl of Albemarle, 24th August, 1833.

" COUTTS & Co."

Within this paper was enclosed the following, in the handwriting of my brother, with his seal:—

"Oct. 20, 1842.

"In the event of my death or incapacity of acting by illness, I place all papers relating to Mrs. Fitzherbert at Coutts's, the bankers, or in any other place, entirely under the control and disposition of my Brother, the Hon. Charles Langdale.

"Witness my hand and seal,

"STOURTON."

However this paper might show the wishes of Lord Stourton, there could be no question as to its invalidity as a legal instrument. I, however, sent a copy of it to Messrs. Coutts, and received from them the following reply:—

"Strand, 18th Dec., 1846.

"SIR,

"We are honoured with your letter of yesterday's date, enclosing a copy of a document signed by Lord Stourton, purporting to give you the control and disposition of some papers left with us.

"The packet to which it refers was left with us by

the late Mrs. Fitzherbert, to be held at the disposal of
the Earl of Albemarle and Lord Stourton, and we
apprehend that the decease of the latter nobleman
places it at the absolute control of Lord Albemarle.

         " We have the honour to be,

             " Sir,

           " Your most obedient,

             " Humble servants,

               " COUTTS & Co."

"THE HON. CHARLES LANGDALE."

I also wrote the following letter to the Duke of
Wellington, and addressed a copy of it, with a few
verbal alterations, to the Earl of Albemarle :—

               " Dec. 1846.

" I take the liberty of informing your Grace, that on
the death of my Brother, Lord Stourton, on the 4th
instant, a parcel of papers was found addressed to me.
These papers refer, at great length, to the connection
of the late Mrs. Fitzherbert with his late Majesty
King George the Fourth. They also comprise several
letters from the Earl of Albemarle and two from your
Grace on the subject of certain documents left in the

hands of Messrs. Coutts and Co., in a sealed packet, and endorsed with the names of your Grace, the Earl of Albemarle, and Lord Stourton.

"In reference to this packet my brother has left a paper, of which I have the honour to enclose a copy. Your Grace will, perhaps, excuse me for adding, that my Brother's papers include a letter addressed to me, expressing a confidence that I will preserve and dispose of these details and correspondence with all discretion towards the public, and regard for the interests of religion and of the character of Mrs. Fitzherbert, &c.

"I beg to assure your Grace, that, having accepted from my lamented Relative during his life this confidential and delicate trust, I have now no other object than that mentioned in his letter. As the safe custody of the documents left with Messrs. Coutts will be the best security for those purposes, an acquiescence on the part of your Grace and the Earl of Albemarle in the wishes expressed by my Brother in the enclosed paper, as far as admitting me to the trust occupied by him, will fully satisfy all my sense of duty to the delicate position in which this delegated confidence has placed me.

(Signed, &c.)   "CHARLES LANGDALE."

To this letter I received the following replies from the Duke of Wellington and the Earl of Albemarle :—

"Strathfieldsaye, Dec. 20, 1846.

"SIR,

"I have had the honour of receiving your letter of the 17th instant. I had before heard of the loss sustained in the person of the late Lord Stourton.

"I have a perfect recollection of the circumstances which you mention, including the sealed packet of papers at Messrs. Coutts, under the seals of Lord Stourton, the Earl of Albemarle, and myself.

"The control over the papers vested in Lord Albemarle is greater than that vested in myself. But I will consent to any arrangement which Lord Albemarle may advisedly suggest.

"I have the honour to be, Sir,

"Your most obedient humble Servant,

"WELLINGTON."

"THE HON. CHARLES LANGDALE,

No. 10, Mansfield Street,

Cavendish Square, London."

The Earl of Albemarle wrote as follows:—

"Berkeley Square, 18th Dec., 1846.

"DEAR SIR,

"I am suffering from an infirmity of sight, which disables me at present from attending to any business in which reading or writing is concerned. As the letter with which you have honoured me relates to a subject of a nature peculiarly delicate, and private, I should be obliged to you to let me have a personal interview with you, and I will wait upon you in Mansfield Street, on Monday, at any hour that you may appoint after two o'clock.

"I have the honour to be,

"Dear Sir,

"Your faithful Servant,

"ALBEMARLE."

"HON. CHARLES LANGDALE."

In reply to my note, accepting his proposal, I received the following:—

"DEAR SIR,

"I shall be happy to meet you either in this house, or in Mansfield Street, between two and three on Monday, whichever may be most convenient to you.

" I have the honour to be,

" Your faithful Servant,

"ALBEMARLE."

" HON. CHARLES LANGDALE.

Saturday."

My interview with Lord Albemarle took place, on the day appointed, at his Lordship's house in Berkeley Square. According to a short note recording the result of this interview, committed by me to paper the same day, I received a promise that the documents at Coutts's should not be removed from their custody without informing me. Lord Albemarle further expressed himself painfully sensible of the trust now vested solely in himself, but had received no reply from the Duke of Wellington, who was out of town, on the subject of my communication. He would try to see him when he came to town.

Such, then, was the position in which I found myself at the close of last year, after the pages of Lord Holland's Memoirs had been pointed out to me, impeaching the reputation of a virtuous Lady, not only connected with me by relationship, and endeared to all who knew her by her personal character, but one whose honour and virtue I had pledged myself to my Brother to defend, in conformity with that same anxious confidence which she had reposed in him.

Had I required other and further motives, I felt myself called upon to justify the conscientious fulfilment of a contract, not only, as will appear, sanctioned by the Church, but to which, under peculiar circumstances, the Church almost enjoined her to adhere.

The question then arose how this defence was to be undertaken.

It appeared, clearly, that the defence which had been made by Lord Stourton had altogether failed in producing, at least, any permanent effects, for the very grounds of his defence were made the argument for founding a fresh charge against her whom he had thus vainly attempted to protect.

What, then, could I hope from any course of a similar description, or from any letter, whenever or however addressed, to the noble editor of his Father's Memoirs? It appeared to me, that if the character of Mrs. Fitzherbert was to be effectually rescued from the attacks aimed at it through those pages, and if there was any hope of securing it from misrepresentation for the time to come, it would only be, by laying before the public such a full and detailed account of the whole course of this Lady's connection with King George the Fourth, as would bear on the face of it the proof of authenticity, and thus not only place before the world at large her own conduct and motives, but also show the part which the Church took in the recognition of her Marriage.

Under these impressions, the first step I took was, to inquire into whose possession the documents deposited at Coutts's had fallen on the death of Lord Albemarle, which had taken place some time previously. I felt, not very unnaturally I think, that these papers, which had been especially preserved by Mrs. Fitzherbert, and placed at the disposal of trustees for the defence of her character, ought now to be made available for this purpose. And it must be admitted, that I, nearly related as I was by blood, professing also the same religious principles as the distinguished Lady who had constituted the trusts,—pledged, moreover, to one of these trustees, named by herself, I may say to that one most identified with all the responsibilities of the trust,—to defend the character, both of this Lady and the religion which she pro-

fessed, made no unreasonable demand, if not actually a
legal one, to the executor of the surviving trustee, into
whose hands a law had consigned the custody of the
papers, to have these preserved papers, or at least a
copy of them, placed at my disposal.

The correspondence below will show the character
of the application made by me to the Hon. and Rev.
Edward S. Keppel, the executor under the will of
the late Earl of Albemarle, and the result of such
application :—

" Houghton, Nov. 16, 1854.

" REV. SIR,

" Understanding that you were, by the will of the late
Lord Albemarle, appointed his executor and trustee,
I take the liberty of addressing you on a subject lately
brought under my notice, in ' The Memoirs of the
Whig Party, by the late Lord Holland, edited by his
Son.' I allude to the connection formed between
George the Fourth, when Prince of Wales, and Mrs.
Fitzherbert.

" Lord Holland thus refers to Mrs. Fitzherbert (p. 141,
vol. ii.), and, as he says, on the authority of a friend,
' a man of strict veracity : '—' I believe, therefore, she
spoke with truth, when she frankly owned that she
had given herself up to him, trusted to his honour,

and set no value on the ceremony which he (the Prince
of Wales) insisted on having solemnised.'

"You will observe, that this involves a direct charge
against the honour and religious principles of Mrs.
Fitzherbert. You may probably be aware, that the
late Lord Albemarle, and the late Lord Stourton (my
Brother), were entrusted by Mrs. Fitzherbert with
certain documents referring to her connection with
George the Fourth. These were deposited in a box
under their seals; and, with the cognisance and seals
of the Duke of Wellington and Sir William Knighton,
as executors of George the Fourth, were committed to
the charge of Messrs. Coutts and Co., Bankers.

"On the death of my Brother, Lord Stourton, in
1846, I waited on the late Lord Albemarle, and informed his Lordship, that I had, at the request of my
Brother, accepted the responsibility of defending the
reputation and religion of Mrs. Fitzherbert, by all
means in my power, should they be assailed from any
quarter whatsoever; that to enable me to do this
effectually, Lord Stourton had placed in my hands a
detailed account of Mrs. Fitzherbert's connection with
George the Fourth, as detailed by Mrs. Fitzherbert
herself; and finally, that, as far as he could, by his
wishes, expressed under his hand and seal, he had con-

stituted me as his successor in the trust deposited with Messrs. Coutts.

"I was aware, as I informed the late Lord Albemarle, that those wishes of my Brother, however clearly expressed, could not legally confer on me the power of a co-trustee; but that from the other documents and correspondence in my possession, I considered myself not only empowered, but bound to my Brother and our estimable friend and relative Mrs. Fitzherbert, to rebut any charge that might be brought against her fair name and character.

"The late Lord Albemarle expressed himself deeply sensible of the importance of the documents of which he was now the sole legal surviving trustee, and finally promised that the box and papers should not be removed from Messrs. Coutts's Bank without previously acquainting me.

"This was all that I could at that time desire, as no aspersions had then rendered it requisite that any other course should be adopted. Unhappily this is no longer the case: Mrs. Fitzherbert is charged, under the high authority of the late Lord Holland, with sacrificing her honour and her virtue to the importunity of the then Prince of Wales, regarding the

ceremony which took place between them as ' nonsense,' &c.*

" Had the late Lord Albemarle been still living, I
cannot admit a doubt, that his Lordship would at once
have made available the documents committed to the
joint charge of his Lordship and the late Lord Stourton, for the special purpose of giving the most authentic
and solemn proofs of the importance which Mrs. Fitzherbert had always attached to her conscientious union
with the Prince of Wales. As having morally, if not
legally, succeeded to the charge which my brother
had accepted, conjointly with the late Lord Albemarle,
I feel myself now bound in honour, as well as in
justice, to rebut the direct charge contained in these
Memoirs, and to denounce the 'veracity' of the informant, be he who he may, who has thus calumniated
to Lord Holland the virtue and religious principles
of an estimable and strictly conscientious Lady.

"It is under these circumstances that I have now
the honour of addressing you as the representative of
the late Lord Albemarle; and as the existence of
documents under the seals of Lords Albemarle and
Stourton as trustees, and of the Duke of Wellington

* Page 141, vol. ii.

and Sir William Knighton as witnesses, are now matters of notoriety, I would beg leave to suggest that the time is now arrived, when they should be made available for the purposes for which they have been preserved.

"As it is my intention to lay before the public a more detailed account of Mrs. Fitzherbert's connection with George the Fourth, when Prince of Wales, than has yet appeared, I would beg to propose that a copy of the preserved documents should be placed at my disposal, the more effectually to establish the grounds upon which the friends and relations of this Lady have ever maintained her full and fair claim to their respect and esteem, and to the character of an honourable and religious woman.

"I have the honour to remain,

"Rev. Sir,

"Your obedient Servant,

"CHARLES LANGDALE."

"THE HON. AND REV. EDWARD S. KEPPEL."

To which I received the following reply:—

"Quidenham, Attleborough, Nov. 29, 1854.

"SIR,

"I must beg you to accept my apology for not ac-

F

knowledging your letter bearing date the 16th instant
sooner, but I have felt the importance of your application, and hesitated to comply with it, until I had
consulted some one whose position and station in life
and judgment might guide me to a right decision.
I have not at present had the opportunity of talking
over the circumstances with any one, and therefore
hope you will not press me for a few weeks to come
to a decision. The packet you refer to is safe at
Coutts's; the seals at present unbroken. My own
opinion, I may add, is, that an unfair aspersion has
been made on Mrs. Fitzherbert's character by the late
Lord Holland, and now published by his son. I have
by me copies of my father's correspondence with the
late Duke of Wellington, your Brother, and yourself,
and I hardly see how the claim now made can be
rejected; but I must beg for time.

" I am, Sir,

" Faithfully yours,

"EDWD. S. KEPPEL."

" Hon. Charles Langdale."

To this letter I replied :—

"Houghton, Brough, Yorkshire, Dec. 4, 1854.

"REV. SIR,

"I can have no objection to a few weeks' delay in repelling the attack directed against the character of Mrs. Fitzherbert. I must, however, observe that it is important the defence should not be too long delayed. Perhaps you will excuse me, if I repeat that the object of the preservation of certain documents, under the sanction of the parties whose seals are affixed to the box at Messrs. Coutts's, was the protection of Mrs. Fitzherbert's character *now* assailed.

"I am,
"Rev. Sir,
"Your obedient Servant,
"CHARLES LANGDALE."
"REV. EDWARD S. KEPPEL."

To this letter, not having received any further reply, on the 16th February I wrote as follows :—

"Houghton, Feb. 16, 1855.

"REV. SIR,

"I hope that you will not consider me very importunate in now requesting to know the course you propose to pursue regarding the papers reserved for the defence of the late Mrs. Fitzherbert's reputation. I feel that I ought not longer to defer fulfilling the pledge which I gave to my Brother, and I trust that, as now the sole legal trustee, you will aid me as far as the reserved papers may do so. I go to-morrow, for a week or ten days, to London, where I hope to hear from you. My address will be Crawley's Hotel, Albemarle Street.

"I am, Sir,

"Your obedient Servant,

"CHARLES LANGDALE."

"HON. AND REV. EDWARD S. KEPPEL."·

To this letter I received the following reply:—

"Quidenham, Feb. 23, 1855.

"SIR,

"I thank you for having given me so much time to consult with others respecting the advisable course for me to take in the proper disposal of the papers depo-

sited at Messrs. Coutts's by the late Mrs. Fitzherbert.
The friend with whom I have been in conference by
letter is the Duke of Bedford, and through him I have
the opinion of the executors of the late Mrs. Fitzherbert, Sir G. Seymour and Mr. Forster. They are
strongly against the production of those papers. They
would only prove the Marriage of the Prince with Mrs.
Fitzherbert, which is not questioned, as Lord Holland's
remarks go to the motives and feelings of herself and
the Prince, which the evidence in the papers would not
touch. The public might, or might not, be interested
in the production of the papers, but the revival of the
subject would, if it attracted interest, only pander to the
bad feelings or the curiosity of the great world, without
doing good, where it is sincerely intended. The public
mind is at rest on the subject, and might it not be advisable to let it rest so ? I think the opinion of the
above parties should have weight.

" I am, Sir,

" Truly yours,

" EDWD. S. KEPPEL."

" THE HON. CHARLES LANGDALE."

My reply to the above communication I here subjoin :—

"March 13th, 1855.

"REV. SIR,

"I beg to acknowledge the receipt of yours, with the opinions of the Duke of Bedford and of the executors of the late Mrs. Fitzherbert on the subject of the papers reserved by that Lady, and entrusted to the late Earl of Albemarle and the late Lord Stourton, for the vindication of her honour, should it be impugned after her death.

"That the honour of this Lady, and her religious principles, have been grossly impugned by a statement of the late Lord Holland, in the papers published by his son, is sufficiently notorious, and, indeed, is admitted in a previous letter from yourself.

"The nobleman and gentlemen whom you have consulted would appear to consider this of minor importance, than the revival of a subject, which might "pander to the bad feelings or curiosity of the great world; that the public mind is at rest on the subject, and that it might be advisable to let it rest so." That the parties consulted should have come to this conclusion, though at the sacrifice of the fair reputation of this injured Lady, does not, indeed, quite surprise me; but I have

taken upon myself obligations which will not allow me
so easily to dispos of the fair fame of a Lady whose
honourable principles I have pledged myself to defend,
and which I am not prepared so readily to abandon to
an insulting charge, even though at the cost of what a
great world may say or think, or even at the risk of
damage to Royal reputation.

" That the reserved papers were intended for such a
purpose, and that the trustees to whose charge they
were committed received them with such an understanding from her whose property they were, you must
excuse me if I confidently repeat. The refusal to
place them at my disposal, only renders it the more
imperative upon me to lay before the public the
whole detail of the connection between Mrs. Fitzherbert and George the Fourth, then Prince of Wales,
as narrated by herself to the late Lord Stourton;
and which, without the reserved documents, will, I
trust, show to the world, that whatever the conduct
of George the Fourth may have been, that of Mrs.
Fitzherbert, under trials of no ordinary description, was
such as to have done honour to the purity of her character as a woman, and to her principles as a Catholic.

" As in any course which I may deem it expedient to
take, reference will necessarily be made to the docu-

ments which have formed the subject of our correspondence, you cannot, of course, object that its purport should be made public.

"I am,

"Dear Sir,

"Your obedient Servant,

"CHARLES LANGDALE."

"THE HON. AND REV. EDWARD S. KEPPEL."

To this letter I received the following reply:—

"Quidenham, Attleborough, March 28, 1855.

"SIR,

"In reply to your letter of the 13th instant, allow me
to say, that I cannot object to your making public, as
you propose, the purport of our correspondence; and can
only regret that I have, with the advice of others, not
felt myself at liberty to comply with your wishes in all
respects. I repeat, that the papers should have been
at your disposal, had they afforded any contradiction to
Lord Holland's imputations. He does not dispute the
fact of the Prince's Marriage with Mrs. Fitzherbert, so
the documents (as far as I can judge from the memo-

randum of their contents, which I have in my possession) cannot answer Lord Holland and his ungracious
imputation. These can only be rebutted by their own
inherent unreasonableness.

                    " I am,
                        " Sir,
                            " Faithfully yours,
                                "EDWD. S. KEPPEL."
"HON. CHARLES LANGDALE."

Having thus failed in obtaining possession of the
papers reserved by Mrs. Fitzherbert, and placed under
the control of trustees, as it appeared to me specially
for the purpose for which I applied for them, it only
remained for me to consider what steps I should take,
not only to supply any deficiency of information arising
from the absence of these documents, but so completely
to establish every fact connected with the transactions
to which they relate, that no further reference could
be made to them, without the public at large being
in full possession of all the circumstances from which
they might be enabled fairly to form a judgment, as to
the course which Mrs. Fitzherbert had pursued, and as
to the grounds on which she acted.

I am free to acknowledge, that, during the lifetime

of this Lady, delicacy would have prevented, even at any cost of malignant calumnies, her personal approval of being thus brought before the eyes of the public in many of the more private relations in which she was connected, both before and after her Marriage, with the Prince of Wales. But that to which a sacrifice during life may be made, can no longer be tolerated, when it is attempted to affix a stigma on the memory of the dead. All minor considerations of delicacy must then yield before the paramount duty to the memory of a woman, to establish her full and fair title to the virtue of chastity. That such was Mrs. Fitzherbert's just prerogative, grounded upon the strictest dictates of her conscience, and supported by the principles of her religion, and sanctioned by the decision of her Church, I am bound at all hazards to establish. To this I consider myself pledged: this I owe to the memory of the dead—this I owe to the cause of virtue, truth, and religion; and, at any personal risk of imputations, of what nature soever, or from what quarter soever, this I am prepared, without reserve, to undertake.

The period to which the publication of these pages has been deferred, but too truly proves that which I am free to acknowledge—not a doubt as to the duty, not a hesitation as to the course—but a repugnance to appear thus in print before the public.

Circumstances have, indeed, contributed to this delay longer than might otherwise have been the case. I had proceeded some way in the task which I have imposed upon myself, when my writing-case, containing my manuscript, of which I had no copy, was stolen from me, and I had to recommence that in which I had, with some trouble and much cost of inclination, considerably advanced.

But had I even doubted, had a hope, however fallacious, encouraged me to adopt the suggestion of the concluding lines of Mr. Keppel's letter, that "the ungracious imputations of Lord Holland can only be rebutted by their own inherent unreasonableness," and that, therefore, I might at least depend upon the malicious calumny of the unnamed informant being limited to the lately-published Memoirs, the last few months have but too truly proved the trite observation as to the sure and rapid propagation of every scandalous story; inasmuch as, on the authority of Lord Holland, the infamous charges of his veracious friend have been reproduced, with the usual advantage of accompanying epithets, which too well show the efficacy of the poison circulated in the original libels.

The author of the Lives of the Queens of the House of Hanover says, in the Introduction to his work: *—" Whenever I could find an eyewitness, I have allowed him to speak, and occasionally at some length, for I question if one could narrate what Ulysses saw better—that is, more truly—than Ulysses himself."

On this principle the author transcribes Lord Holland's story, that it was the Prince of Wales, and not Mrs. Fitzherbert, who insisted upon the Marriage ceremony being performed. " Mrs. Fitzherbert, however, frankly enough said, that the ceremony would be all nonsense, and that she was ready to trust to his honour." The addition, that this was on the faith of an unnamed friend of Lord Holland, " a man of strict veracity," is, however, left out, and the naked fact is stated as one of unquestioned notoriety. Accordingly, this writer does not hesitate elsewhere to place Mrs. Fitzherbert in the same category as a debauched actress. " Mrs. Crouch, the actress, and Mrs. Fitzherbert, were the Lucy and Polly to whom this light-of-heart Prince gaily sang his ' How happy could I be with either !' "

Now, supposing this author to adopt as true the

* " Lives of the Queens of England of the House of Hanover," 2 vols. Second Edition, 1855.

alleged quotations from Lord Holland, I am far from wishing to condemn the parallel drawn between a Lady, however differing in rank and worldly esteem, and the poor despised actress. I am at a loss, indeed, to know what these impugners of the character of Mrs. Fitzherbert can mean, or what they may suppose that she herself meant, by what they quote as her words, " trusting to his honour," in the same breath that she avows having dishonoured herself. On these suppositions I can make no distinction between the victims of lawless passion ; but were I inclined to do so, it should be in favour of the poor seduced actress over the lady of rank and fashion, where either the Marriage ceremony was indeed considered nonsense, or where, as unfortunately for the character of George the Fourth, there was not even the semblance of such sanction. But in this publication, insulting as it is in its inferences against the character of Mrs. Fitzherbert, there is what Mr. Keppel styles the same " inherent unreasonableness " from the quotations which he selects from other works, as well as Lord Holland's ; all show-ing not only the respect paid by the Royal Family generally, but a noble assertion of the rights of a wife, and a self-respect in public demeanour, equally opposed to, and incompatible with, the character of guilt.

Indeed, Dr. Doran appears to feel the force of this, when he observes, upon certain extracts from the "Diary" illustrative of the Court of George the Fourth, that they evince "a judgment which abounds in a confusion of terms, and exhibit a mental perversion in him who pronounced it." This "Diary" is quoted as stating of Mrs. Fitzherbert, that she "had a stronger hold over the Regent than any of the other objects of his admiration, and that he always paid her the respect which her conduct commanded." Certainly, here is confusion of terms and mental perversion enough, if all the respect which she could command was that which was due to an abandoned wanton.

Again, the "Diary" pronounces Mrs. Fitzherbert to have been "the most faultless and honourable mistress that ever a prince had the good fortune to be attached to."

If by the term "mistress" crime is implied, well may Dr. Doran complain of confusion in the epithet of honour attached thereto; and if the good fortune of a prince consists in successful debauchery, he can hardly too strongly comment on such mental and moral perversion.

But the following extracts from the "Diary" are too creditable to the then Prince of Wales not to be gladly

added to these pages. " It should be added," says Dr.
Doran,* " that the intelligence no sooner reached the
ears of the Queen than she commanded the attendance of her son, and insisted on knowing the whole
truth. The Prince is declared not only to have acknow-
ledged the fact of the Marriage, but to have asserted that
no power on earth should separate him from his wife.
He is reported to have added, in reference to the
King's alleged marriage with Hannah Lightfoot, that
his father would have been a happier man had he
remained firm in standing by the legality of his own
marriage. It would be difficult to say who was at
hand to take down the Prince's speech on this occasion ; but, according to the author last named, it was
substantially as follows :—' But I beg farther that my
wife be received at Court, and proportionately as your
Majesty receives her, and pays her attention from this
time, so shall I render my attentions to your Majesty.
The lady I have married is worthy of all homage, and
my very confidential friends, with some of my wife's
relations only, witnessed our Marriage. Have you not
always taught me to consider myself heir to the first
sovereignty in the world? Where, then, will exist any

* "Lives of the Queens of England of the House of
Hanover."

risk of obtaining a ready concurrence from the House in
my Marriage? I hope, madam, a few hours' reflection
will satisfy you, that I have done my duty in following
the impulse of my inclinations, and therefore I await
your Majesty's commands, feeling assured that you
would not blast the happiness of your favourite
Prince.' The Queen is said to have been softened by
his rather illogical reasoning. It is certain, that Her
Majesty received Mrs. Fitzherbert, at a drawing-room
in the following year, with very marked courtesy.

"Sixteen years later, and, of course, long after the
Marriage of the Prince of Wales with Caroline of
Brunswick, Mrs. Fitzherbert was still so high in the
Prince's favour that we find the following record in
Lord Malmesbury's Diary, under the date of May 25,
1803:—'Duke of York came to me at five. Uneasy
lest the Duchess should be forced to sup at the same
table with Mrs. Fitzherbert, at the ball to be given by
the Knights of the Bath, on the 1st of June. Talks it
over with me; says the King and Queen will not hear
of it. On the other side, he wishes to keep on terms
with the Prince. I say, I will see Lord Henley, who
manages the fête, and try to manage it so that there
shall be two distinct tables; one for the Prince, to
which *he* is to invite, another for the Duke and

Duchess, to which *she* is to invite her company.'
The dislike of Mrs. Fitzherbert for the Duchess of
York was as determined as that entertained by the
same lady against Fox, whom she never forgave for
denying the fact of her Marriage with the Prince."
Now, once more, how does all this accord with
Mrs. Fitzherbert's alleged repudiation of the Marriage
ceremony between herself and the Prince, and that
" she had given herself up to him—trusting to his
honour?"

Here, then, is the course which charges, however
deeply affecting character, but too usually run. One
noble Lord writes Memoirs, and therein tells an in-
credible story on the authority of some friend, of whose
" veracity " he says he entertains a high opinion. The
noble son publishes these Memoirs to the world, tales
and all, however damaging to the fair name of a Lady
avowedly esteemed and respected by the highest and
brightest of the country. Then comes the writer who
collects, from every available source, the best information, and relates it in the language, and rests its
authenticity on the faith, of others.

In answer to all this, I now proceed to present Mrs.
Fitzherbert's own account of her connection with George
the Fourth, when Prince of Wales; and as I purpose to

give it full and entire, as delivered by the Lady herself to a near relative and attached friend, whose name
shall vouch for the truthfulness of the narration as
delivered to him, I cannot but hope, that on the face
of these hitherto private circumstances of the relationship between Mrs. Fitzherbert and the Prince, there
will be stamped such a character of authenticity, as to
place on lasting record the events themselves, as well
as the circumstances and motives which preceded, accompanied, closed, and, I may venture to say, justified
them.

It is indispensable, however, for me previously to
lay before the reader the correspondence between the
parties concerned in depositing the sealed documents
with Messrs. Coutts. The character of these documents will, in a great degree, compensate for the refusal
on the part of the executors of the late Earl of Albemarle to place the papers themselves at my disposal.

It has already appeared, in my communication with
the Hon. and Rev. Edward Keppel (to whom, upon the
death of Lord Albemarle as surviving trustee of Mrs.
Fitzherbert, the trust of those papers devolved as executor to the late Earl), that I claimed the right of
making any use I might think expedient of these preserved papers,—preserved for the very purpose for

which I put in my claim; not, indeed, a legal claim, as I have before admitted, but a moral right, to judge how far they might aid in establishing, once for all, the fair fame of the Lady who, in her anxiety to maintain it untainted by the breath of reproach, had consigned these treasured documents to the keeping of her dearest friends and near relatives.

In support of this view, I think I can safely appeal, not only to portions of this correspondence, on the part of Mrs. Fitzherbert's trustees, but also, as reported by Lord Albemarle to Lord Stourton, to a letter, dated February 1, 1841, by the Duke of Wellington, strongly as he protested against opening the sealed paper, in another communication from himself to Lord Stourton. Lord Albemarle thus reports the sentiments expressed by the Duke of Wellington :—" There was not now, nor had there been, any attack upon Mrs. Fitzherbert's reputation. *Did any appear in any quarter, he would be eager in joining us to repel it.*"

Lord Albemarle's letter to Lord Stourton, dated April 6, 1837, on the death of Mrs. Fitzherbert, which had then recently occurred, sufficiently shows how sensitive this noble Lord was to the trust reposed in him, and how anxious he was promptly to take any steps which might be serviceable in regard to the documents confided to his care. The advisers, indeed, of the Hon. and Rev. Gentleman take a different view of the expediency of moving in the matter ; and, rather than arouse public attention to these bygone events, are willing to consign the character of an innocent and injured woman to the obloquy which her contemporaries would have thought it only a bare act of justice to repel. Sympathising with these kinder feelings, I will enable the public to judge between us, by laying before them the sentiments entertained on the subject (as far as the same may be collected from the correspondence which took place) by the principal actors concerned in these transactions.

"The Stud House, August 10, 1833.

"DEAR LORD STOURTON,

"I have much pleasure in informing you, that our business is drawing towards a satisfactory termination. After two interviews with the Duke of Wellington, we have agreed, subject to your approbation, to the proposed terms, which I direct to you under another cover. Mrs. Fitzherbert is, I believe, *perfectly* satisfied. I have had the honour of submitting to the King* a full statement

* King William the Fourth.

of the whole case, and his Majesty gives his cordial sanction to the proposed arrangement. It, however, waits for your approval; and should anything occur to you as neglected, or incautiously guarded, have the goodness to let me know. The Duke of Wellington takes it upon his own responsibility that Sir William Knighton shall retain no papers whatever, and the word *knowledge* in the proposal does not mean any restraint over our disposition of the papers retained, but merely that the other party shall not be taken by surprise by our publication of them without notice. I think it a word useless to be inserted, but of no consequence.

" I have been commanded by the King to invite Mrs. Fitzherbert to dine with him on Saturday, the 24th, and also your Lordship, to meet her on that day, should it happen that you are in London.

" Believe me,

" Dear Lord Stourton,

" Sincerely yours,

"ALBEMARLE."

" Correct Copy,
    STOURTON."

" It is agreed by Mrs. Fitzherbert on the one part, and

the executors of the late King on the other, that each will destroy all papers and documents (with the exception of those hereafter mentioned) in the possession of either, signed or written by Mrs. Fitzherbert, or by her. directions, or signed or written by the late King, when Prince of Wales, or King of Great Britain, &c., or by his command. The two parties agree, that in case any papers signed or written by either of the parties above mentioned, or by the authority of either, shall ever hereafter be found among the papers of the other, they shall be given up as the property of the writer or signer thereof, or of the person who authorised the writing or signature thereof. Such papers and documents as Mrs. Fitzherbert shall wish to keep, shall be sealed up in a cover under the seals of the Duke of Wellington and Sir William Knighton, and of the Earl of Albemarle and Lord Stourton, and be lodged in the bank of Messrs. Coutts, at the disposition of the Earl of Albemarle and of Lord Stourton. The seals not to be broken without the knowledge of the Duke of Wellington and Sir William Knighton. It is understood that no copy of any paper or document is to be taken or kept on either side."

Here follows a list of the papers and documents retained by Mrs. Fitzherbert :—

" 1. The Mortgage on the Palace at Brighton.

" 2. The Certificate of the Marriage, dated Dec. 21st, 1785.

" 3. Letter from the late King, relating to the Marriage, signed [George the Fourth].

" 4. Will written by the late King [George the Fourth].

" 5. Memorandum written by Mrs. Fitzherbert, attached to a letter written by the clergyman who performed the Marriage Ceremony.

" Correct Copy,

" STOURTON."

" An exact copy. Witness my hand,

"STOURTON."

" Berkeley Square, June 5, 1837.

"DEAR LORD STOURTON,

"I hope the words of the endorsement, of which I forward a copy, will fully answer the object desired.

" Very faithfully yours,

" ALBEMARLE."

In the handwriting of Lord Stourton, but added
" not exact Copy :"—

" I entirely concur in the proposal transmitted to
me by the Earl of Albemarle, and give my sanction
to any mode that Mrs. Fitzherbert and Lord Albemarle may deem expedient for carrying it into effect.
I will affix my seal to the parcel containing the reserved documents on my return to town, and I now
authorise the Earl of Albemarle, with the concurrence
of Mrs. Fitzherbert, to destroy the rest.

" I would only observe, that ' the *knowledge*' of the
Duke of Wellington and Sir William Knighton, Bart.,
is not understood to make them of necessity *consent-
ing parties* to the inspection of the reserved papers to
be deposited at Coutts's Banking-house,—and I will
take the liberty of suggesting, whether it might not be
advisable, for the clear understanding of the parties,
and to avoid any future misapprehension, that Mrs.
Fitzherbert should be consulted as to the future appointment of Trustees under this trust, but liable to
the same limitations to the appointment of herself,
whether by herself during life, or by the Earl of
Albemarle and Lord Stourton, should they survive her;
or the death of any other parties whose sanction or

privity is required by the proposal, might perhaps be construed against the friends of Mrs. Fitzherbert into a surrender of the papers.

" I tender these suggestions, leaving it to Mrs. Fitzherbert and the Earl of Albemarle to give them only such weight as they may think they possess, and fully concurring in their decision.

" Witness my signature,
"STOURTON."

" The Stud House, August 25.

" DEAR LORD STOURTON,

" The difficulty of finding the Duke of Wellington unengaged, and that alone, has caused the delay.

" I am happy in being able to inform you, that the business is now completely arranged, and, I believe I may add, to the satisfaction of all parties. Yesterday, the Duke of Wellington, Mrs. Fitzherbert, and myself, were busily engaged in burning all the letters on either side, with the exception of those which Mrs. Fitzherbert chose to keep. It would be unjust to the Duke of Wellington, if I did not say that his conduct was gentlemanly and friendly to Mrs. Fitzherbert in every respect, and I know that she is perfectly satisfied.

"After our great work of burning was over, I went to Messrs. Coutts's, and delivered into Mr. Dickie's hands (by Mrs. Fitzherbert's desire) the parcel containing the documents and letters reserved, signed and sealed by the Duke of Wellington and myself. Whenever your Lordship returns to London you will have the goodness to add your name and seal.

"It is satisfactory to me to add, that amongst the papers brought and destroyed by the Duke of Wellington, were the letters which Mrs. Fitzherbert had missed, and which she supposed to have been obtained by Sir William Knighton, and kept by him. I believe the letters were of no consequence, but I clearly saw that this circumstance was an additional relief to Mrs. Fitzherbert's mind. I am sure we both cordially agree in the hope, and I trust I may add in the confidence, that her anxiety on this most delicate subject may now be entirely set at rest. She expresses most feelingly her gratitude to your Lordship for your useful and zealous assistance.

"Believe me, dear Lord Stourton,

"Sincerely yours,

"ALBEMARLE."

"Correct Copy,
  "STOURTON."

In the handwriting of Lord Stourton, but added, "not exact Copy:"—

"DEAR LORD ALBEMARLE,

"Under the propitious auspices of your Lordship, I confidently anticipated the favourable issue to which you have brought Mrs. Fitzherbert's concerns, and I am happy to hear that she is satisfied with the result. I think Mrs. Fitzherbert retains everything essential to the protection of her character and property; and it must be a solid consolation that His Majesty has been graciously pleased to interest himself in, and to sanction, an arrangement which, while it protects the parties, shelters them at the same time from unnecessary publicity.

"May I request your Lordship to make known to His Majesty my due sense of the honour he was so condescending as to confer upon me by his commands to meet Mrs. Fitzherbert at dinner on the 24th, and to make the proper apologies on account of absence from town.

"With respect to the agreement which your Lordship has enclosed, I would only suggest one circumstance, that, as the Marriage, however illegal, is considered by our Church as valid, whether Mrs. Fitz-

herbert might not be advised to write at the back of
the certificate, 'No issue from this Marriage.

"' Witness my hand,

"' M. F—H—RT.'

"I offer this suggestion on two grounds: the 1st,
on historical grounds, that in all after-times it may
be known there was no such issue; the 2nd, that it
will render the document more valuable, and, consequently, more likely to be preserved. I merely make
the suggestion, but place no consequence upon it, if
either Mrs. Fitzherbert or yourself see any objection.
I beg my kind regards to her; and will you be kind
enough to acquaint her, that I could come to town if
she desired it, but I feel I could be of no use, as your
Lordship has my entire sanction, and any friend of
Mrs. Fitzherbert might be authorised by me to sign
and seal the preserved papers, as well as to satisfy the
Duke of Wellington and Sir William Knighton of the
destruction of the others. But, at the same time, I
beg my fair Cousin will command any services she may
require.

"Your Lordship possessing at once the friendship of
Mrs. Fitzherbert and the confidence of His Majesty, is
all that can be requisite to carry your own successful

negotiation to a close in its details; and if you and
Mrs. Fitzherbert will allow me to be, which I could
only be from the first, a sleeping partner in the firm, I
shall not, I beg your Lordship to believe, be less grateful on my own part, for having enabled us to bring
this delicate business to a termination alike beneficial
to all."

"Berkeley Square, April 6, 1837.

"DEAR LORD STOURTON,

"A duty connected with much delicacy, and perhaps
also with much difficulty, has fallen upon us by the death
of our much-valued friend Mrs. Fitzherbert. There
have been already some articles in the newspapers,
particularly in the "Times" yesterday, and notices of
publication of Memoirs, &c., which may call for our
interference. I earnestly hope your Lordship will soon
be in London, that the benefit of your advice and the
sanction of your judgment may be made serviceable to
the charge confided to us. It appears to me, that the
first step taken is of fearful importance, and it may
also be necessary that it may be taken promptly. It
would not be right for me to act alone, nor dare I do
it. I cannot help repeating my earnest hope that you

may be able to be in London; and in the meantime
have the goodness to communicate to me anything
which your judgment may suggest to you as right to
be done.

> " I have the honour to be,
>> " My dear Lord,
>>> " Very faithfully yours,
>>>> " ALBEMARLE."

" Correct Copy,
>> " STOURTON."

" MY DEAR LORD,

" I had penned a note to your Lordship when I was
last in town, but the alarming illness of my mother
called me into the country at an hour's notice, and the
same cause continuing prevented my return; or I should
ere this, have again troubled your Lordship about Mrs.
Fitzherbert's papers. I do not feel satisfied that we
have done everything required, till I am cognisant of
the nature of the document signed 5 in our Memorandum, said to contain · a Memorandum written by
Mrs. Fitzherbert, attached to a letter written by the
clergyman who performed the Marriage ceremony.

" Of all the Documentary Papers, I consider this

probably the *most* important; particularly, if I am correct in the notion that this Memorandum contains Mrs. Fitzherbert's testimony that no issue arose from this Marriage. At all events, the clergyman's letter is, in itself (particularly as the Certificate is a mutilated instrument), a valuable record in favour of our friend's reputation. I had myself, previously to this arrangement, taken the liberty to counsel Mrs. Fitzherbert to leave some evidence in her own handwriting as to the circumstances of no issue arising from this connection, and had advised it being noted with her own signature at the back of the Certificate. To this she smilingly objected, on the score of delicacy, and I only state it at present in justification of my expectation that the Memorandum I have alluded to is to this effect. Be it as it may, I cannot rest satisfied that I have entirely fulfilled my duty towards my relative and friend, while I remain in entire ignorance of the exact purport of this clergyman's letter and the attached Memorandum.

" I may take an erroneous view of this matter, but having taken it, I am confident that your Lordship will be the first to excuse my pressing it upon you. I am aware that these papers at Coutts's cannot be opened without the ' knowledge ' of his Grace the Duke of

Wellington, though 'placed by Mrs. Fitzherbert at Messrs. Coutts's, also at the disposal of the Earl of Albemarle and Lord Stourton, according to a Memorandum dated the 24th August, 1833.'

" I am also aware that his Grace expressed much reluctance to the breaking of the seals, when I applied, since Mrs. Fitzherbert's death, for the opening of the parcel, and that I was myself induced, however reluctantly, to yield to his Grace's suggestions, and to leave the documents for the time undisturbed. The Duke of Wellington assumed, that Mrs. Fitzherbert herself had shown an indisposition to disturb and re-open this parcel, and therefore that her friends could not, and ought perhaps not, to be more watchful over her character than she had been herself. I ventured I think, at the moment, in the interview I had the honour of receiving at Apsley House with his Grace, to state, that my acquaintance with Mrs. Fitzherbert's sentiments as to these papers was wholly at variance with the views so entertained by his Grace.

" But the Duke of Wellington may now evince less objection to *our* seeing, or *to your Lordship alone* inspecting, and giving me an account of the letter and adjoined Memorandum, for this would satisfy me. And in pursuance of this object, I authorise your Lordship to break the seal affixed by myself, either *in the presence* of his Grace the Duke of Wellington, or *not.*

" Since my interview with his Grace on this business, I have felt obliged, by a sense of duty, to contradict, in my own name, the statements in the *Edinburgh Review* (with the knowledge of their author), and I have been appealed to by a court of law, by a Judge of the land, in testimony of no child being born from this *illegal* Contract. I have, moreover, in common with his Grace, been appealed to by an impostor,* assuming to have been the issue of this connection. I have, therefore, various grounds to desire to know all essential particulars respecting papers confided to our joint care and disposition.

" The Duke stands upon *other* grounds, and represents other interests. Should his Grace say, that he cannot allow those seals to be broken without informing the Highest Personage in the country, as he informed us on our last application during the lifetime of William the Fourth, be it so. These Documents were placed at our disposition, with *the express sanction* of William the Fourth; and I cannot assume that her present Majesty will decline sanctioning any claims springing

* To this person I have never replied, nor ever intended to do so.

H

from a sense of duty in the fulfilment of a delicate
and important trust.

"I subjoin an extract from one of the letters
I have preserved; and, I may add, that my very
last communication with Mrs. Fitzherbert related to
these papers; but it was destroyed when read, as it
merely referred to our deliberations at our next meeting in town, which her death soon after prevented.
My knowledge, as I have before informed your Lordship, that her end was wholly unexpected by herself
for some days which preceded it, until she was *wholly
unequal* to take cognisance of *any* business whatsoever,
will account for no further notice.   This information I
received from the Roman Catholic clergyman, Don
Lopez, her private chaplain.   The following is the
extract alluded to:—'I have seen Lord Albemarle
frequently, and told him the contents of your letter
respecting your seal, in case the papers should be removed from Coutts's; but as you had left town, and as
you were the chief person I wished to consult about
them, I have, *for the present*,* desired Lord Albemarle
not to make any application to the Duke of Wellington till some future occasion.'

* Underlined by myself, and not by Mrs. Fitzherbert.

" I have not the exact date of this quotation, but the black edge, and the mention of Mr. Craven, the Dowager Marchioness of Downshire's death, and her return from abroad, sufficiently mark the time, and her intention of not leaving these papers FINALLY at Coutts's.

" A further question still must obtrude upon us, and I shall at any time be glad to receive your Lordship's sentiments upon it. What is to become eventually of these papers? Mrs. Fitzherbert assigned her reasons to me for not placing them either under the custody of the Damers or the Jerninghams; and did me the honour, as probably she also consulted your Lordship, of advising with me respecting them; but this is a more remote question, and even the Memorandum I want to see may offer some suggestion.

" The first question is, and to that I cannot reply in any manner quite satisfactory to myself, what these papers are? Your Lordship will, therefore, pardon me for again troubling you and, through your Lordship, his Grace the Duke of Wellington, to satisfy me on this point. Believe me, my dear Lord, nothing but the sense of a sacred obligation to the memory of a confiding friend would render me thus

importunate. This long letter (I wish, for your Lordship's sake, I could have abridged it satisfactorily
to myself) is entirely at your disposal, to send or
not to the Duke—at your entire command; and I
shall hope his Grace will see the necessity for my observations, and his own ability to comply with them, as
far at least as your Lordship's inspection, without any
difficulty on his part.

> " I have the honour to remain,
> " My Lord,
> " Your Lordship's obliged
> " and obedient Servant,
> "STOURTON."

> "Berkeley Square, February 1, 1841.

" DEAR LORD STOURTON,

" The Duke of Wellington's engagements, as well as
my own official duties at the beginning of the Session,
have prevented me from putting forward the wish contained in the letter with which you honoured me about
a week ago, till Saturday, when I called upon his Grace,
and submitted your letter to his attention. He was

particularly kind and courteous in his manner, and read your letter with great attention. He then requested me to state to you, that he felt he had a public duty as well as a private one to perform, in keeping the papers alluded to, if possible, undisturbed, on account of their importance; that there was not now, nor had there been, any attack upon Mrs. Fitzherbert's reputation. Did any appear in any quarter, he would be eager in joining us to repel it; that all was well now. However, he was very unwilling to raise any difficulty in your way to satisfy yourself upon every particular that you wished, and when you arrived in London he hoped to have the opportunity of talking over the subject with you in the most friendly dispositions.

" The Duke added, that he thought the other point in your letter, respecting the future disposal of the papers, deserved very serious consideration, and he was very anxious to discuss this matter when your Lordship came to London, and we could all be present together.

"I have no political news to report. There seems to be at present a calm, probably however to be soon broken by a storm, but from what quarter no one seems to know. Perhaps Lord Stanley's Irish Legislation Bill may make a beginning to-morrow. However, the intentions of the Opposition are kept secret.

" I have the honour to be,

" My dear Lord,

" Very faithfully yours,

" ALBEMARLE."

" LORD STOURTON,

" &c., &c."

" Walmer Castle, August 10, 1841.

" MY LORD,

" When the late Mrs. Fitzherbert desired to receive from those who had possession of the papers of the late King George the Fourth, under authority of His Majesty's last Will, all papers written by herself, or relating to herself, I considered that I performed a duty towards His then late Majesty George the Fourth, towards the Sovereign on the throne, and the Royal Family, as well as to Mrs. Fitzherbert, and the public at large, by submitting to that Lady the proposition that all papers in the possession of those who had charge of the King's papers under authority of his last Will, which related to Mrs. Fitzherbert, or were written or signed by herself, on the one hand, and all those in possession of Mrs. Fitzherbert which related to the late King George the Fourth, or were written or signed by himself, on the other, should be delivered up and destroyed in presence of the parties having possession of the same; which was carried into execution accordingly at Mrs. Fitzherbert's house in Tilney Street, in presence of Mrs. Fitzherbert, myself and others, with the exception as follows:—

" Mrs. Fitzherbert expressed a strong desire to retain undestroyed particular papers in which she felt a strong interest. I considered it my duty to consent to these papers remaining undestroyed, if means could be devised of keeping them as secret and confidential papers as they had been up to that moment.

" Mrs. Fitzherbert expressed an anxiety at least equal to that which I felt, that those papers, although preserved, should not be made public.

" It was agreed, therefore, that they should be deposited in a packet, and be sealed up under the seals of the Earl of Albemarle, your Lordship, and myself, and lodged at Messrs. Coutts's, the bankers.

" Circumstances have, in some degree, changed since the death of Mrs. Fitzherbert; but it is still very desirable to avoid drawing public attention to, and re awakening the subject by, public discussion of the narrations to which the papers relate, which are deposited in the packet sealed up, to which I have above referred. And I am convinced that neither I nor any of the survivors of the Royal Family, of those who lived in the days in which these transactions occurred, could view with more pain any publication or discussion of them than would the late Mrs. Fitzherbert when alive.

" Under these circumstances, and having acted conscientiously and upon honour throughout the affairs detailed in this letter, I cannot but consider it my duty to protest, and I do protest most solemnly, against the measure proposed by your Lordship, that of breaking the seals affixed to the packet of papers belonging to the late Mrs. Fitzherbert, deposited at Messrs. Coutts, the bankers, under the several seals of the Earl of Albemarle, your Lordship, and myself.

" I have the honour to be,

" My Lord,

" Your Lordship's most faithful

" and obedient humble Servant,

" WELLINGTON."

" The Lord Stourton,
Allerton Park."

I subjoin two other letters from the Duke of Wellington on the subject:

" To THE EARL OF ALBEMARLE.

"My coming to town will probably not be early in the season unless urgent business should compel me; but I could not delay longer writing to your Lordship."

" Dec. 10, 1841."

"London, April 22, 1842.

" F. M. the Duke of Wellington presents his compliments to Lord Stourton. His Lordship is mistaken. The Duke does not fill any office in Her Majesty's political service, or at Her Majesty's Court. As a member of the Privy Council, he has for some months been summoned to attend Her Majesty's councils; but not filling any office, he has no power or authority. He cannot obtrude his advice upon Her Majesty, unless in the Privy Council, or unless his advice should be required by Her Majesty.

"Lord Stourton will probably be of opinion that there has been no alteration in the situation of the Duke of Wellington since the late correspondence between his Lordship and the Duke upon the subject

of Mrs. Fitzherbert's papers. The Duke requests that
Lord Stourton will excuse him for declining at this
moment to appoint a time at which he could receive
Lord Stourton.

" The business in Parliament, and other public business to which it is the Duke's duty to attend, occupy
his whole time. He is anxious, therefore, to postpone
the honour of receiving his Lordship, till a more
advanced period of the Session; at which time, it
appears by his Lordship's note, that he wishes to see
the Duke in the presence of the Earl of Albemarle
and others.

" THE LORD STOURTON,

No. 10, Mansfield Street,

Cavendish Square."

To the above letters I think it may be interesting
to the reader, and therefore desirable, to add the following four from Mrs. Fitzherbert herself. They are
addressed to Lord Stourton ; and, from the confidential
and affectionate tone in which they are written, will
corroborate the interesting communications which that
noble Lord elsewhere details as having received from
this distinguished Lady.

I.

MY DEAR LORD STOURTON,

Don't think me ungrateful. You would do me much injustice, if you could for a moment suspect me of not feeling all I owe to you for your kindness, and the trouble I have given you; but I have been suffering so much from a very severe attack of illness, which has confined me nearly five weeks to my room, that I have been perfectly incapable of attending to anything. I told Lord Albemarle how uncomfortable I was at not having been able to write to you, and he promised me you should be informed of everything from him. I long to talk it over with you whenever it pleases God that I may again have the happiness of seeing you.

My medical advisers tell me the best chance I have is to go into another climate, and I propose setting out in a day or two for Aix-la-Chapelle. My mind being more at ease, I trust I may enjoy a little better health than I have done. I cannot expect at my time of life to be free of all ailments, and I must submit and be thankful for the many kind friends I have met with to support me in all my difficulties; to none do I feel more indebted than yourself. Excuse this horrid scrawl; but the moment I was able to use my pen I was determined to express to you, my dear Lord Stourton, not only the gratitude, but the very sincere regard and affection of

"Yours most truly,

"M. FITZHERBERT."

II.

"Paris, Dec. 7, 1833.

"MY DEAR LORD STOURTON,

"I have taken up my pen twenty times with the intention of writing to you to enquire after you, but the fear of appearing troublesome has always prevented my pestering you with a letter; though I feel much rather that you should think me troublesome, than for a moment suspect me of ingratitude, or of not bearing constantly in my mind the kind interest you have taken in my affairs. I know I must have been a great torment to you, but I am sure the kind feelings of your heart will derive some gratification, in having relieved me from a state of misery and anxiety which has been the bane of my life; *and I trust, whenever it shall please God to remove me from this world, my conduct and character (in your hands) will not disgrace my family and my friends.*

"I wrote a few lines to you before I left London, where I remained very unwell, and worried to death with business of all sorts. I went to Aix-la-Chapelle; the waters did wonders; and I found my health so improved by change of scene, that I determined to pass my winter on the Continent somewhere in the south of France. But everything being in a state of confusion and uncertainty, I resolved to come here, where everything is perfectly quiet: should it be otherwise, it is so near England that I might easily return, which I could not do if I were at a great distance.

" I have taken a very quiet apartment and live very retired, seeing occasionally some friends. The Duke of Orleans came to see me the moment I arrived, with a thousand kind messages from the King and Queen, desiring me to go to them, which I accordingly have done. Nothing could exceed the kindness of their reception of me: they are both old acquaintances of mine. I have declined all their fêtes, and they have given me a general invitation to go there every evening whenever I like it, in a quiet family way, which suits me very much. I really think I never saw a more amiable family: so happy and so united. The King seems worn to death with business all day and all night; but he assured me that things were going on much better, though there were a great many wicked people trying to make mischief. I told him that I was afraid he had sent many of them to make disturbance in our country. He is very much attached to England, and hopes we shall always be friends.

" Your affectionate,

" M. FITZHERBERT."

III.

" Brighton, Oct. 9, 1834.

"MY DEAR LORD STOURTON,

" I have had my pen in my hand several times to write to you, but since my arrival the change of climate, and the overpowering weather we have had lately, has made me unfit for anything. Thank God! I am now getting quite well again.

" I cannot tell you how much I regretted on my return not to find you in London. I arrived much later than I intended, and was fearful you had left for the country, and that I should not be able to have the pleasure of seeing you. I trust, however, it will not be very long before we meet. I have a thousand things to talk to you about, and should anything bring you to town pray let me know.

" I am going to make a visit to my two nieces, Lady Bathurst and Mrs. Craven, and I shall return here for the winter. But I fear I could not tempt you to visit Brighton, which would give me very sincere pleasure could I hope there was a chance of seeing you here.

" The King sent for me a day or two after I got to London. Nothing could be more kind than his reception, and he made me a very handsome present, which he said he had had made purposely for me, but would not *send it during my stay on the Continent.*

" I inclose you a letter I received about a week ago from your son William.

" May I beg you to say everything most kind from me to Lady Stourton; and allow me, dear Lord Stourton, to assure you of my best wishes, and of the sincere regard and affection of,

" Your very grateful and much obliged,

" M. FITZHERBERT."

IV.

" MY DEAR LORD STOURTON,

" I have taken up my pen very often to write to you, but for the last fortnight so many very melancholy occurrences have assailed me, and my spirits have been so oppressed, that I have been fit for nothing.

" The tragical and sudden death of poor Mr. Craven has left my poor niece in a state of wretchedness not to be described. Two such young and happy people scarcely existed. He only twenty-five, and she just completed her twenty-second year—left with two little children.

" Four days after this sad event I had the misfortune to lose one of the oldest friends I had, in the death of poor Lady Downshire. I write you these details, well knowing the kindness of your nature, that you will make allowances for my having been so long in acknowledging the kind letter you were so good as to send me some weeks ago.

" I have seen Lord Albemarle frequently, and told him the contents of your letter respecting *your seal*, in case the papers should be removed from Messrs. Coutts; but as you had left town, and as you were the chief person I wished to consult about them, I have for the present desired Lord Albemarle not to make any application to the Duke of Wellington till some future occasion. Lord Albemarle says you have written a most excellent letter, accompanied with your subscription to O'Connell, and that your party are highly delighted with it. I shall make no comments upon it, except that I think the *O.* and the *Ex.* both very mischievous people.

" I hope you have good accounts of your son William, and that you will have the pleasure of seeing him soon.

" I beg my best regards to Lady Stourton, and everything kind from me to the rest of the family, and that you will believe me,

" My dear Lord,

" Your grateful and affectionate,

" M. FITZHERBERT."

Lord Stourton prefaces the Narrative, which I now proceed to lay before the public, with a curious anecdote of the infant years of Mrs. Fitzherbert.

" Attentions from Royalty, as I have heard Mrs. Fitzherbert say, as if to prognosticate her future destinies, commenced with her at a very early age. Having accompanied her parents, while yet a child, to see the King of France at his solitary dinner at Versailles, and seeing Louis the Fifteenth pull a chicken to pieces with his fingers, the novelty of the exhibition struck her fancy so forcibly, that, regardless of Royal etiquette, she burst into a fit of laughter, which attracted the Royal notice, and His Majesty sent her a dish of sugarplums by one of his courtiers. The bearer of this Royal present was the Duke de Soubise, as she afterwards heard from himself, who well remembered the circumstance; and it is rather a curious coincidence, in her connection with Royalty, that the last dregs of bitterness were presented to her from a Royal table connected with a French Sovereign, Louis the Eighteenth.

At the close of the following Narrative, Lord Stourton adds:—" Publication will depend upon the necessity for doing so, to vindicate the character of Mrs. Fitzherbert and her religion." Committed, then, as this manuscript was, to me, with this condition attached, the foregoing pages will have sufficiently shown to the reader the grounds upon which I have come to the conclusion, that, upon both the above motives, the necessity for such publication has now arrived.

LORD STOURTON'S NARRATIVE.

" About to give to the public some particulars relating to the eventful life of this distinguished

Lady, I wish to preface these observations with one or two reflections; namely, that my object in doing so, is not to gratify public curiosity, but solely to vindicate the memory of a virtuous woman from past or future aspersions detrimental to her fame. In performing this duty, I shall be governed by a desire to bring nothing into view that I can deem superfluous, or which can hurt unnecessarily the feelings of others: such particulars only as are essential to the ends of justice, and for exhibiting Mrs. Fitzherbert's conduct through life in that pure and true light in which it has appeared to myself, and to which she had every right to urge her claim. To do more, would be to act in contradiction to her own declared and deliberate wishes, and to my own acts and suggestions in being a party to the destruction of all letters and documents not intimately connected with the just representation of her long irreproachable, and interesting history. To do less, would be, I am convinced, not to realise the expectations or fulfil the trust reposed in me in communications the most confidential and unreserved.

" In the midst of the afflictions, both of body and mind, which weighed down the latter years of the life of Mrs. Fitzherbert, the thought which most soothed her pains and assuaged her grief, was, the consoling

testimony which would be borne to her character
when she should be no more ; when, all the actors in
this extraordinary drama being removed by the hand
of death, the veil might be drawn aside which had
prompted secrecy during her life ; and her character
might be shown to posterity in the light in which
it appeared to herself, unsullied by crime, and even
untarnished by interesteaness or ambition. With
this view she almost insisted, in our confidential communications, upon my requiring from her every information respecting her conduct from her first connection with George the Fourth down to his death—
as evidence to satisfy my mind of the strictest propriety of every portion of her conduct that I might
deem doubtful or objectionable.

" After disclosures so intimate, and to my judgment so satisfactory, I should not wish to descend
into the tomb myself, leaving her reputation to
the doubtful testimony of others less informed, even
if equally disposed to render her justice. Associated
with some, in the custody of a few important
papers relative to her history, I stand single in a
nearer relationship to this distinguished personage in
some important and intimate connections, and was,
therefore, probably selected by her on that account, to

be honoured with communications of so very delicate and confidential a nature. Having deliberately accepted the proffered confidence, ·I should not feel happy to leave to the chances of ill-advised or mercenary biographers the portraiture of one so difficult to pencil in her true and accurate lineaments.

" Mrs. Fitzherbert was first acquainted with the Prince when residing on Richmond Hill, and soon became the object of his most ardent attentions. During this period she was made the subject of a popular ballad, which designated her under the title of the 'Sweet Lass of Richmond Hill:'—

> "' I would crowns resign to call her mine,
> Sweet lass of Richmond Hill.'

She was then the widow of Mr. Fitzherbert, in possession of an independent income of nearly 2,000l. a year, admired and caressed by all who were acquainted with her character and singular attractions.

" Surrounded by so many personal advantages, and the widow of an individual to whom she had been sincerely attached, she was very reluctant to enter into engagements fraught with so many embarrassments, and, when viewed in their fairest light, exposing their object to great sacrifices and difficulties. It is not, therefore, surprising that she resisted, with the utmost anxiety and firmness, the flattering assiduities of the most accomplished Prince of his age. She was well aware of the gulf that yawned beneath those flattering demonstrations of royal adulation.

"For some time her resistance had been availing, but she was about to meet with a species of attack so unprecedented and alarming, as to shake her resolution, and to force her to take that first step, which afterwards led by slow (but on the part of the Prince successful) advances, to that union which he so ardently desired, and to obtain which he was ready to risk such personal sacrifices. Keit, the surgeon, Lord Onslow, Lord Southampton, and Mr. Edward Bouverie, arrived at her house in the utmost consternation, informing her, that the life of the Prince was in imminent danger—that he had stabbed himself—and that only *her* immediate presence would save him. She resisted, in the most peremptory manner, all their importunities, saying that nothing should induce her to enter Carlton House. She was afterwards brought to share in the alarm, but still, fearful of some stratagem derogatory to her reputation, insisted upon some lady of high character accompanying her, as an indispensable condition; the Duchess of Devonshire was selected. They four drove from Park Street to Devonshire House, and took her along with them. She found the Prince pale, and covered with blood. The sight so overpowered her faculties, that she was deprived almost of all consciousness. The Prince told her, that nothing would induce him to live unless she promised to become his wife, and permitted him to put a ring round her finger. I believe a ring from the hand of the Duchess of Devonshire was used upon the occasion, and not one of his own. Mrs. Fitzherbert being asked by me, whether she did not believe that some trick had been practised, and that it was not really the blood of His Royal Highness, answered in the negative; and said, she had frequently seen the scar, and that some brandy-and-water was near his bedside when she was called to him on the day he wounded himself.

"They returned to Devonshire House. A deposition was drawn up of what had occurred, and signed and sealed by each one of the party, and, for all she knew to the contrary, might still be there. On the next day, she left the country, sending a letter to Lord Southampton, protesting against what had taken place, as not being then a free agent. She retired to Aix-la-Chapelle, and afterwards to Holland. The Prince went down into the country to Lord Southampton's for change of air.

"In Holland, she met with the greatest civilities
from the Stadtholder and his family, lived upon terms of
intimacy with them, and was received into the friendship of the Princess of Orange, who, at that very time,
was the object of negotiation with the Royal Family
of England for the Heir Apparent. Frequent inquiries
were made about the Prince and the English Court
in confidential communications between her and the
Princess, it being wholly unknown to the Princess that
she was her most dangerous rival. She said she was
often placed in circumstances of considerable embar-
rassment; but her object being to break through her
own engagements, she was not the hypocrite she might
have appeared afterwards, as she would have been very
happy to have furthered this alliance. She afterwards saw this Princess in England, and continued
to enjoy her friendship, but there was always a great
coolness on the part of the Stadtholder towards her.

"She left Holland in the Royal Barge, and spent
above another year abroad, endeavouring to 'fight off'
(to use her own phrase) a union fraught with such
dangerous consequences to her peace and happiness.
Couriers after couriers passed through France, carrying the letters and propositions of the Prince to her
in France and Switzerland. The Duke of Orleans

was the medium of this correspondence. The speed of the couriers exciting the suspicion of the French Government, three of them were at different times put into prison. Wrought upon and fearful, from the past, of the desperation of the Prince, she consented, formally and deliberately, to promise she would never marry any other person; and lastly she was induced to return to England, and to agree to become his wife, on those conditions which satisfied her own conscience, though she could have no legal claim to be the wife of the Prince.

" I have seen a letter of thirty-seven pages, written, as she informed me, not long before this step was taken, entirely in the handwriting of the Prince; in which it is stated by him that his Father would connive at the union. She was then hurried to England, anticipating too clearly and justly, that she was about to plunge into inextricable difficulties; but, having insisted upon conditions, such as would satisfy her conscience and justify her in the eyes of her own Church, she abandoned herself to her fate. Immediately after her return she was married to the Prince, according to the rites * of the Catholic Church in this

* I do not imagine that by using the term "rites of the Catholic Church," it is intended to imply that the Roman

country; her uncle Harry Errington and her brother
Jack Smythe being witnesses to the contract, along
with the Protestant clergyman who officiated at the
ceremony. No Roman Catholic priest officiated. A
certificate of this Marriage is extant in the handwriting of the Prince, and with his signature, and
that of Mary Fitzherbert. The witnesses' names were
added; but at the earnest request of the parties, in a
time of danger, they were afterwards cut out by Mrs.
Fitzherbert herself, with her own scissors, to save
them from the peril of the law.

"This she afterwards regretted; but a letter of the
Prince on her return to him, has been preserved to
supply any deficiency, in which he thanks God, that
the witnesses to their union were still living; and
moreover, the letter of the officiating Clergyman is
still preserved, together with another document with
the signature and seal, but not in the handwriting, of
the Prince, in which he repeatedly terms her his wife.

"The first signal interruption to this ill-fated engagement arose from the pecuniary difficulties of His

Ritual, and the ceremonies therein prescribed, were followed
on the occasion; but that such forms and circumstances were
observed, as were recognised by the Catholic Church to be
substantially required for the Marriage Contract.

Royal Highness, when, on the question of the payment of his debts, Mr. Fox thought himself justified by some verbal or written permission of the Prince, to declare to the House of Commons that no religious ceremony had united the parties. This public degradation of Mrs. Fitzherbert so compromised her character and her religion, and irritated her feelings, that she determined to break off all connection with the Prince, and she was only induced to receive him again unto her confidence, by repeated assurances that Mr. Fox had never been authorised to make the declaration; and the friends of Mrs. Fitzherbert assured her, that, in this discrepancy as to the assertion of Mr. Fox and the Prince, she was bound to accept the word of her husband. She informed me, that the public supported her by their conduct on this occasion; for, at no period of her life were their visits so numerous at her house as on the day which followed Mr. Fox's memorable speech; and, to use her own expression, the knocker of her door was never still during the whole day.

"I told her, that I understood there was a scrap of paper from the Prince to Mr. Fox; that Sir John Throckmorton, a friend of his, had assured me of the fact of the Prince wishing much to obtain possession

of it, but though written on a dirty scrap of paper,
it was much too valuable to be parted with. She
said that she rather doubted the fact. I think the
difference between the assertions of the Prince and Mr.
Fox may be accounted for under a supposition (which
I have also heard) either that there was some ambiguity in the expressions used, or that Mr. Fox might
have referred to what had passed antecedently at
Devonshire House, without being privy to their subsequent more formal engagements.

" However this may be, an accommodation took
place between Mrs. Fitzherbert and the Prince, though
she ever afterwards resolutely refused to speak to Mr.
Fox. She was, however, obliged sometimes to see him,
and was much urged by the Prince to a reconciliation;
but, though of a forgiving disposition upon other occasions, and even benefiting some who most betrayed her
confidence, she was inflexible on this point, as it was
one of the only means left her to protect her reputation.
She thought she had been ill-used in a most unjusti-
fiable manner by this public declaration before the
House of Commons; especially as she had been waited
upon by Mr. Sheridan, who had informed her, that
some explanation would probably be required by Parliament on the subject of her connection with the

Heir Apparent. She then told him, that they knew she was like a dog with a log round its neck, and they must protect her. She went so far with respect to Mr. Fox, that when afterwards, during his administration, he made some overtures to her in order to recover her good-will, she refused, though the attainment of the rank of Duchess was to be the fruit of their reconciliation. On naming this circumstance to me, she observed that she did not wish to be another Duchess of Kendal.

"Her first separation from the Prince was preceded by no quarrel or even coolness, and came upon her quite unexpectedly. She received when sitting down to dinner at the table of William the Fourth, then Duke of Clarence, the first intimation of the loss of her ascendancy over the affections of the Prince; having only the preceding day received a note from His Royal Highness, written in his usual strain of friendship, and speaking of their appointed engagement to dine at the house of the Duke of Clarence. The Prince's letter was written from Brighton, where he had met Lady Jersey. From that time she never saw the Prince, and this interruption of their intimacy was followed by his marriage with Queen Caroline; brought about, as Mrs. Fitzherbert conceived, under the twofold influence of the pressure of his debts on the mind of the Prince, and a wish on the part of Lady Jersey to enlarge the Royal Establishment, in which she was to have an important situation.

" Upon her speaking to me of this union (confiding in her own desire that I should disguise from her nothing that I might conceive to be of doubtful character as affecting her conduct to the Prince), I told her I had been informed that some proposals had been made to her immediately preceding the marriage of the Prince, of which her uncle, Mr. Errington, had been the channel, offering some terms upon which His Royal Highness was disposed to give up the match. She told me there was no truth whatever in the report; that a day or two preceding the marriage he had been seen passing rapidly on horseback before her house at Marble Hill, but that his motive for doing so was unknown to her; and that afterwards, when they were reconciled, she cautiously abstained from alluding to such topics; as the greatest interruptions to their happiness, at that period, were his bitter and passionate regrets and self-accusations for his conduct, which she always met by saying—'We must look to the present and the future, and not think of the past.'

" I ventured also to mention another report, that

George the Third, the day before the marriage,
had offered to take upon himself the responsibility
of breaking off the match with the Princess of
Brunswick, should the Prince desire it. Of this, too,
she told me she knew nothing, but added that it was
not improbable, for the King was a good and religious
man. She owned, that she was deeply distressed and
depressed in spirits at this formal abandonment, with
all its consequences, as it affected her reputation in
the eyes of the world.

" One of her great friends and advisers, Lady
Claremont, supported her on this trying occasion, and
counselled her to rise above her own feelings, and to
open her house to the town of London. She adopted
the advice, much as it cost her to do so; and all the
fashionable world, including all the Royal Dukes,
attended her parties. Upon this, as upon all other
occasions, she was principally supported by the Duke of
York, with whom, through life, she was always united
in the most friendly and confidential relations. Indeed,
she frequently assured me, that there was not one of
the Royal Family who had not acted with kindness to
her. She particularly instanced the Queen; and, as
for George the Third, from the time she set footing in
England till he ceased to reign, had he been her own

father he could not have acted towards her with greater
tenderness and affection. She had made it her constant
rule to have no secrets of which the Royal Family
were not informed by frequent messages, of which the
Duke of York was generally the organ of communication, and to that rule she attributed at all periods
much of her own contentment and ease in extricat-
ing herself from embarrassments which would otherwise have been insurmountable.

" When she had thought her connection with the
Prince was broken off for ever by his second union,
she was soon placed by him in difficulties from the
same earnest and almost desperate pursuit as she
had been exposed to during the first interval of his
attachment. Numbers of the Royal Family, both
male and female, urged a reconciliation, even upon a
principle of duty.

" However, as she was, by his marriage with Queen
Caroline, placed in a situation of much difficulty, in-
volving her own conscience, and making it doubtful
whether public scandal might not interfere with her
own engagements, she determined to resort to the
highest authorities of her own Church upon a case of
such extraordinary intricacy. The Rev. Mr. Nassau,
one of the chaplains of Warwick Street Chapel, was,

therefore, selected to go to Rome and lay the case
before that tribunal, upon the express understanding,
that, if the answer should be favourable, she would
again join the Prince; if otherwise, she was determined
to abandon the country. In the meantime, whilst the
negotiation was pending, she obtained a promise from
His Royal Highness that he would not follow her
into her retreat in Wales, where she went to a small
bathing place. The reply from Rome, in a brief which
in a moment of panic she destroyed, fearful of the consequences during Mr. Percival's administration, was
favourable to the wishes of the Prince; and, faithful
to her own determination to act as much as possible
in the face of the public, she resisted all importunities
to meet him clandestinely. The day on which she
joined him again at her own house, was the same on
which she gave a public breakfast to the whole town
of London, and to which he was invited.

"She told me, she hardly knew how she could
summon resolution to pass that severe ordeal, but she
thanked God she had the courage to do so. The next
eight years were, she said, the happiest of her connection with the Prince. She used to say that they
were extremely poor, but as merry as crickets; and
as a proof of their poverty, she told me that once, on

K

their returning to Brighton from London, they mus-
tered their common means, and could not raise 5*l.*
between them. Upon this, or some such occasion, she
related to me, that an old and faithful servant endeavoured to force them to accept 60*l.*, which he said he
had accumulated in the service of the best of Masters
and Mistresses. She added, however, that even this
period, the happiest of their lives, was much embit-
tered by the numerous political difficulties which frequently surrounded the Prince, and she particularly
alluded to what has been termed 'the delicate investigation,' in which Queen Caroline and His Royal
Highness had been concerned.

" Sometimes family jealousies, as in the case of the
Duke of York, in the Prince's letter to the King,
were subjects of great anxiety, in which she always
endeavoured to heal any differences which occurred.
Indeed, she said that the two Princes were much
attached to each other though the Prince of Wales
was frequently jealous of the superior attentions the
Duke of York received from their Royal Father, but
through life the Duke had always acted 'beautifully,'
to use her own expression.

" Upon one occasion, not long before his death, in
alluding to the delicate connection existing between

his brother and Mrs. Fitzherbert, and the political consequences it might involve, he said, 'Thank God, he never could wish to raise any claim in contravention of the rights of his brother.' It was, however, only in the latter part of his life that he had seen the mutilated document which I have termed the certificate of the Marriage.

"A circumstance now took place, which ended by blasting all her happy prospects, and finally terminated in a rupture with the Prince, which lasted till the end of his life. One of the dearest friends of Mrs. Fitzherbert, Lady Horatia Seymour, in the last stage of a decline, was advised to go abroad, to seek in change of climate her only chance of recovery. She had at that time an infant, and not being able to take it with her, she entrusted her treasure to the care of her attached friend Mrs. Fitzherbert, who, having no child of her own, soon became devotedly attached to the precious charge, and her affection for the child increased with the loss of the parent. Some time afterwards one of the near relatives of the family, desirous of having the education of the child placed in other hands, and being jealous of the religion of its protectress, applied to the Chancellor to obtain possession of Miss Seymour, as guardian. Mrs. Fitzher-

K 2

bert, now more than ever devoted to the child, and sharing in this affection with the Prince himself, exerted every means to retain the custody of it, and, after all others had failed, had at last recourse to Lady Hertford, with whom she was formerly intimately acquainted. She requested her to intercede with Lord Hertford, as head of his house, to come to her aid, and, demanding for himself the guardianship of the child, to give it up to her upon certain conditions as to its education.

"This long negotiation, in which the Prince was the principal instrument, led him at last to those confidential relations, which ultimately gave to Lady Hertford an ascendancy over him superior to that possessed by Mrs. Fitzherbert herself, and from a friend converted her into a successful rival. Lady Hertford, anxious for the preservation of her own reputation, which she was not willing to compromise with the public even when she ruled the Prince with the most absolute sway, exposed Mrs. Fitzherbert at this time to very severe trials, which at last almost, as she said, ruined her health and destroyed her nerves. Attentions were required from her towards Lady Hertford herself, even when most aware of her superior influence over the Prince, and these attentions were

extorted by the menace of taking away her child. To
diminish her apparent influence in public as well as
private was now the object. When at Brighton, the
Prince, who had passed part of his mornings with Mrs.
Fitzherbert on friendly terms at her own house, did
not even notice her in the slightest manner at the
Pavilion on the same evenings, and she afterwards
understood that such attentions would have been
reported to her rival.

"She was frequently on the point of that separation
which afterwards took place, but was prevented by
the influence of the Royal Family from carrying her
resolution into effect. Upon one occasion, after the
death of Queen Caroline, upon the Prince informing
her that he was determined to marry again, she only
replied, 'Very well, Sir;' but upon his leaving her,
she ordered horses with a resolution to abandon the
country, and was only prevented from doing so, that
day, by the interposition of a common friend, the same,
I believe, if my memory does not fail me, who was
afterwards the bearer of the last tribute of her
affection and conjugal duty to the King, to which I
shall hereafter have to refer.

" A dinner, however, given to Louis XVIII. brought
matters at last to a conclusion; and satisfied of a systematic intention to degrade her before the public, she

then at last attained the reluctant assent of some of
the members of the Royal Family to her determination
of finally closing her connection with the Prince, to
whom, in furtherance of this decision, she never afterwards opened the doors of her house. Upon all former
occasions, to avoid etiquette in circumstances of such
delicacy as regarded her own situation with reference
to the Prince, it had been customary to sit at table
without regard to rank. Upon the present occasion
this plan was to be altered, and Mrs. Fitzherbert was
informed through her friends at Court, that at the
Royal table the individuals invited were to sit
according to their rank.

"When assured of this novel arrangement, she
asked the Prince, who had invited her with the rest
of his company, where she was to sit. He said,
'You know, Madam, you have no place.' 'None, Sir,'
she replied, 'but such as you choose to give me.'
Upon this she informed the Royal Family that she
would not go. The Duke of York and others endeavoured to alter the preconcerted arrangement, but the
Prince was inflexible; and aware of the peculiar circumstances of her case, and the distressing nature of
her general situation, they no longer hesitated to
agree with her, that no advantage was to be obtained
by further postponement of her own anxious desire to

close her connection with the Prince, and to retire once more into private life. She told me, she often looked back with wonder that she had not sunk under the trials of those two years.

"Having come to this resolution, she was obliged, on the very evening, or on that which followed the Royal dinner, to attend an assembly at Devonshire House, which was the last evening she saw the Prince previously to their final separation. The Duchess of Devonshire, taking her by the arm, said to her, ' You must come and see the Duke in his own room, as he is suffering from a fit of the gout, but he will be glad to see an old friend.' In passing through the rooms, she saw the Prince and Lady Hertford in a tête-à-tête conversation, and nearly fainted under all the impressions which then rushed upon her mind, but, taking a glass of water, she recovered and passed on.

"Thus terminated this fatal, ill-starred connection, so unfortunate, probably, for both the parties concerned. Satisfied as I was with the very full explanation of all the circumstances, and of the propriety and almost necessity of the course which Mrs. Fitzherbert was compelled to pursue, I yet felt, that her intimate relations with the Prince might have imposed upon her some duties during his last illness

the non-fulfilment of which would have left my mind
not fully satisfied. I therefore availed myself again
of the confidence which had been so repeatedly urged
upon me, to inquire of her, whether any communication
had taken place previously to his demise. She told
me ' Yes,' and that she would show me the copy of
a letter which she had written to the King a very
short time before his death, which she said had been
safely delivered by a friendly hand; the person assur-
ing her, that the King had seized it with eagerness
and placed it immediately under his pillow, but that
she had not received any answer. She was, however,
informed that, on the few last days of his life, he
was very anxious to be removed to Windsor Cottage.

"Nothing, she said, had so ' cut her up,' to use her
own expression, as not having received one word in
reply to that last letter. It is true, she observed, that
she had been informed by the Duke of Wellington,
that he more than once expressed his anxiety that a
particular picture should be hung round his neck and
deposited with him in the grave, and it seemed to be
the opinion of his Grace that this portrait was one
which had been taken of her in early life, and was set
round with brilliants. It appeared the more likely, as
this portrait was afterwards missing when the others
were returned to her. The copy of the letter, which,

in answer to my question, she went into her bedroom to fetch, she put into my hands to read. It was an expression of her fears that the King was very ill, and an affecting tender of any services she could render him, in a strain which I could not read without sympathising deeply in her distress.

"Soon after his death she left town for Brighton. There, she a second time received the kindest messages from William the Fourth; but upon his inquiry why she did not come to see him, she stated the peculiar difficulties of her situation, and a wish, if it was not asking too much from his condescension, that he would graciously honour her with a personal communication at her own house, previously to her visit to the Pavilion.

" The King kindly complied with her request without delay, and she told him that she could not, in her present circumstances, avail herself of the honour of waiting upon His Majesty, without asking his permission to place her papers before him, and requesting his advice upon them. Upon her placing in his hands the Documents which have been preserved in justification of her character, and especially the certificate of her Marriage, and another interesting and most affecting paper, this amiable Sovereign was moved to tears by their perusal, and expressed his surprise at so

much forbearance with such Documents in her possession, and under the pressure of such long and severe
trials.   He asked her what amends he could make
her, and offered to make her a Duchess.   She replied,
that she did not wish for any rank ; that she had borne
through life the name of Mrs. Fitzherbert; that she
had never disgraced it, and did not wish to change it;
that, therefore, she hoped His Majesty would accept
her unfeigned gratitude for his gracious proposal, but
that he would permit her to retain her present name.

"' Well, then,' said he, ' I shall insist upon your
wearing my livery,' and ended by authorising her to
put on weeds for his Royal Brother.   He added, ' I
must, however, soon see you at the Pavilion;' and I
believe he proposed the following Sunday, a day on
which his family were more retired, for seeing her at
dinner, and spending the evening at the Pavilion.
' I shall introduce you myself to my family,' said he,
' but you must send me word of your arrival.'

" At the appointed hour, upon her reaching the
Pavilion, the condescending monarch came himself
and handed her out of her carriage, and introduced
her to his family, one after the other, as one of themselves.   He ever after treated her in the same gracious manner, and on one occasion, upon her return
from Paris, made her a present of some jewels, which

he said he had had some time, but would not send them to her abroad, as he wished to give them to her himself on her return to England. He afterwards entered, as I shall proceed to relate, into conversation on matters relating to her dearest interests, and to sanction the custody of such papers as were thought most available in support of her honour and fair reputation with posterity.

" Mrs. Fitzherbert told me, that the first day, when, in compliance with the commands of the King, she went to the Pavilion, and was presented by him to the Queen and Royal Family, she was herself much surprised at the great composure with which she was able to sustain a trial of fortitude which appeared so alarming at a distance; but she believed the excitement had sustained her. It was not so the next dinner at which she was present in the same family circle; and the many reflections which then oppressed her mind very nearly overpowered her. Afterwards she frequently attended the King's small Sunday parties at Brighton, and then, as upon all other occasions, she was received with uniform kindness and consideration.

" Many letters of hers, even when writing from abroad to fight off her marriage, had been preserved

by the King. Some were also in possession of Sir
William Knighton, who had obtained possession of
the King's correspondence, either as being his executor, or from having Colonel MacMahon's letters in
his custody. She had also various letters of her own
from the Prince. It was therefore agreed, by the
friends of both parties, that, with a few exceptions,
the whole correspondence should be destroyed.

" In this arrangement William the Fourth kindly
concurred, and it was carried into effect; only such
papers being preserved as Mrs. Fitzherbert thought
fit to select to bear witness to her character.

" It may be well here to state, that her communications through life were even more confidential with
the Duke of York than with the Duke of Clarence,
and these communications continued without interruption till the day of his death. Messages to George
the Third at one time, and to the Queen at another,
were sent through this friendly medium. Their letters
to each other were of the most confidential kind. The
Duke frequently came to her house, day after day
passing many hours in her company, and entering
with her into all the circumstances of the times.
Their agreement with each other was, never to give
up their authorities, with the exception, which she

always made, that she would observe no secrets to the disadvantage of the Prince, only she promised never, even to him, to divulge the source from whence she derived her information. This she strictly observed, though she was sometimes scolded by the Duke for giving him information, without any authority.

" She owed much of the contentment of her life to the open manner in which she was able, through such a channel, to communicate with the King and Queen on occasions of delicacy to guide her conduct. Such correspondence was always maintained by verbal messages. She always endeavoured to avoid interfering in politics; but at one time, she furthered the earnest wish of the Father to prevent the Son from attending at a Newmarket meeting. At another time, when the greatest coolness subsisted between the Father and the Son, who was not even spoken to at Court, she obtained from the King (knowing how much the Prince suffered from this extreme coolness) a promise to speak with kindness to the Prince, who returned from Court in the highest spirits, unaware of the person to whom he was indebted.

" To the Duke of York and the Queen, Mrs. Fitzherbert was indebted for 6,000*l.* a year in a mortgage deed, which they procured for her on the Palace at

Brighton; being aware, as she said, that till that
period, she had no legal title to a single shilling should
she survive the Prince. Indeed, at one period she
had debts upon her own jointures, incurred principally
on account of the Prince; and when the Duke of
Wellington, as executor to George the Fourth, asked
her if she had anything to show, or claim upon the
personalty of the deceased Sovereign, she told him
she had not even a scrap of paper, for that she had
never in her life been an interested person.

"It is well perhaps likewise to state, that previously to the death of the Duke of York, they
agreed on both sides that all their correspondence
should be destroyed; and she assured me, that when
Sir Herbert Taylor gave her up her own correspondence, she was for two years employed in the perusal
and burning of these most interesting letters. When
Sir Herbert Taylor surrendered them to her in person,
she told him that she had been almost afraid that
they would have got these papers from him. He
replied, 'Not all the kings upon earth should have
obtained them.' She added, that had she entertained
mercenary views, she believed she might have obtained
any price she had chosen to ask, for the correspondence
which it was in her power to have laid before the

public; that she could have given the best private and public history of all the transactions of the country, from the close of the American war down to the death of the Duke of York, either from her communications with the Duke, or her own connections with the opposite party, through the Prince and his friends.

" Upon one memorable exception only she was called upon by the Prince, and, indeed, expressly sent for to Brighton, to give her opinion on a step of great political importance which he was about to take, but her influence then had been some time on the wane. He told her, that he had sent for her to ask her opinion, and that he demanded it of her, with regard to the party to which he was about, as Regent, to confide the administration of the country. At his commands, she urged in the most forcible manner she was able, his adherence to his former political friends. Knowing all his engagements to that party, she used every argument and every entreaty to induce him not to sever himself from them. ' Only retain them, Sir, six weeks in power. If you please, you may find some pretext to dismiss them at the end of that time; but do not break with them without some pretext or other.' Such was her request to him. He answered, ' It was impossible, as he had promised;' but at the same time

she observed he seemed much overpowered by the
effort it cost him. Finding that resistance to a determination so fixed was unavailing, she asked to be
allowed to return to Brighton, which she did; but
previously to leaving him, she said, that as he had
done her the honour of imposing upon her his commands of freely declaring her sentiments upon this
occasion, she hoped he would permit her, before she
left him, to offer one suggestion, which she trusted he
would not take amiss.

"She then urged upon him, as strongly as she was
able, the disadvantages which must accrue to his future
happiness from treating his daughter, the Princess
Charlotte, with so little kindness. ' You now, Sir,'
she said, ' may mould her at your pleasure, but soon
it will not be so; and she may become, from mis-
management, a thorn in your side for life.'   ' That
is your opinion, Madam,' was his only reply.

" I must here also add, that not only with the
Royal Family, but also with the Princess Caroline,
Mrs. Fitzherbert was always on the best terms. As
to the Princess Charlotte, Mrs. Fitzherbert said, the
Prince was much attached to her for some years;
indeed, he was generally fond of children and young
people, and it was only when the Princess Charlotte

became the subject of constant altercation betwixt him and those who took part with Queen Caroline, that he at last began to see her with more coolness. Upon one occasion, Mrs. Fitzherbert told me, she was much affected by the Princess Charlotte throwing her arms round her neck, and beseeching her to speak to her Father, that he would receive her with greater marks of his affection; and she told me that she could not help weeping with this interesting child.

"Indeed, Lady De Clifford was one of Mrs. Fitzherbert's particular friends."

["These forty-one pages were written from my dictation, or copied and carefully revised.

"STOURTON."]

Such is the short summary of the eventful life of Mrs. Fitzherbert in connection with her Marriage with the Prince of Wales, afterwards George the Fourth, as detailed by herself to her friend and relative the late Lord Stourton.

On the legal character of that Marriage which united her in the sight of God and her conscience to the Heir to the Throne, I have already said that it is not my purpose to insist. Every Catholic who has arrived at

L

an advanced period of life, and has entered on the
Marriage state in his earlier years, must have practically felt the distinction between the laws of God and
the enactments of the State.

To legitimate his union, to secure their inheritance
to his children, a Catholic was forced to the foot of
an altar which he repudiated—before a minister of a
religion which he disowned; but the State had made
this a condition of its recognition of the Marriage,
and ignored all the sacred obligations which God
might have sanctioned. I am, however, not inclined
to argue the question of justice or injustice, as far as
the law, in the case of the Prince of Wales, was
likely to be operative; but this I cannot hesitate to
affirm, that where a man is a willing party to a
religious solemnisation of the Marriage contract,
knowing that contract to be binding upon the other
party, and pledging his word as the test of his own
sincerity; and yet on the plea of human legislation
sets at defiance engagements thus formed, such a party
can hardly expect an acquittal in the opinion of any
one to whom either honour or conscience is sacred.

That George the Fourth would have been a better
man, a happier husband, and a more respected Sovereign, had he adhered to those solemn engagements, of

which we are assured he was most earnest in urging
the formation, can hardly be doubted by any one who
considers the motives of his more legal union with the
Princess of Brunswick, or who chooses to inquire into
the more private and still less excusable intimacies of
his after life. It is not, however, my wish, nor is it requisite for
the purpose for which I have published these pages,
to follow up the melancholy results of that subsequent
union according to law, which was notoriously forced
on the Prince of Wales as a means of discharging his
pecuniary obligations. The painful scene of that Marriage ceremony, in which Lord Holland informs us the
Prince was under the influence of stimulants so frequently repeated as almost to disqualify him from going
through it, was, according to the same authority,
"attributed by many at the time to remorse at the
recollection of a similar ceremony which had passed
between him and Mrs. Fitzherbert." Indeed, I have
extracted from the " Memoirs of the Queens of England of the House of Hanover" by Dr. Doran, a
passage strongly corroborative of the sentiments entertained by the Prince of Wales himself as to the
binding character of the engagement which he considered he had contracted with Mrs. Fitzherbert, and

which he urged upon the Queen as a reason for a
recognition of that Lady in the character of his Wife.

" I must, therefore, make one remark on the part
taken by the Parents of this young Prince on the
subject of his subsequent marriage with the Princess
of Brunswick. Considering the avowal made to his
Royal Mother of his prior marriage; considering the
knowledge which his Royal Father must have had of
the same, founded on the assurance which the Prince
himself had given to Mrs. Fitzherbert that the King
would connive at their union ; it is, indeed, lament-
able that they should have been parties almost to the
act of forcing on their son an alliance to which the
innocent Princess could hardly. fail to prove a victim.

A curious anecdote is told of Queen Caroline, in
allusion to the prior marriage of the Prince of Wales
with Mrs. Fitzherbert.

On the occasion of her trial before the House of
Lords, she had made a solemn denial of any criminal
conduct. She afterwards is related to have said, that
she ought to have made one exception to that general
denial, which was her Marriage with the Prince of
Wales.

What the sentiments of Mrs. Fitzherbert were,
what the principles of her religion inculcated, what

the authority of her Church sanctioned, and may even
have been said to have enjoined, when deciding upon
the delicate point of returning to a husband whose
act had, as far as depended upon himself, renounced
his plighted troth, and transferred it to another, the
facts contained in these pages will, I trust, set at rest
for ever.

True to the sacred injunction of the Founder of
her faith—"Whom God has joined, let no man put
asunder"—Mrs. Fitzherbert was instructed that, united
by the sacred and indissoluble tie of Marriage to the
Prince of Wales in the sight of God, human law
might indeed have illegitimated her children, had she
had any, might have carried out the threat denounced
by the Prince's friend and adviser Mr. Fox, of de-
priving him of his succession to the Throne; but
human law could not abrogate the law of God, nor
could any misconduct of her husband emancipate her
from that sacred vow, which her Church taught her
could not be dissolved but by death.

Could any one proof more strong than another
be afforded in refutation of Lord Holland's whole story
of unscrupulous conduct, it is the appeal made by Mrs.
Fitzherbert to Rome, as to her duty, in the peculiar
situation in which she was placed by the second Mar-

riage of the Prince. This Marriage had all the legal
sanction of both King and Parliament, which had been
wanting in a public form to her own union. It had,
as far as the act of man could do it, dissolved the tie
by which she was united to the Heir to the Throne, and
he whom she had taken for her husband had, by this
public act, been himself a party to this transaction.
Well, then, might she hesitate as to what duty prescribed in such a case; when the rights of a husband
were again claimed by him who had so lately transferred his allegiance to another. Friends might, indeed, and, including members of the Royal Family, did
support her; but, as she herself states, public opinion
—the world's judgment—would condemn her. In such
a position, who was to guide her in deciding on the
claims of him whom she owned as her husband before
God, but whom the State had recognised as the husband of another? She appealed to that authority to
which, as a Catholic, she looked as supreme in dic-
tating the law of conscience and of God.

The reader will have seen this decision, recognising,
at one and the same time, the validity of the contract
which had made her the Wife of the Prince of Wales,
and the inalienable right of a husband, as such, to her
restored affections. Accordingly, her own account

records the reunion which in consequence took place,
under which probably the Prince passed the happiest
period of his life.

Every friend of morality must, I think, have read with
pleasure that, at that period at least, George the Fourth
was susceptible of feelings of remorse for conduct which
his conscience told him no human legislation could
justify. But, once more, how idle, in the face of such
conduct on the part of Mrs. Fitzherbert, the charge of
unscrupulous indifference brought by Lord Holland's
friend against this Lady, whose hesitation, in a case
of such peculiar delicacy, nothing less than an appeal
to the highest tribunal of the Church could satisfy!
Indeed, the world at large might, for once, have
been said to take up the cause of God and his holy
law against the enactments of human power. Never
was woman in the ambiguous position in which Mrs.
Fitzherbert was placed by the second Marriage of her
husband, more generally justified by the support and
respect of public opinion. One instance is of so
striking a nature, as connected with the highest
Court of Judicature in the kingdom, that I cannot
forbear adverting to it here, as at once a testimony
to her high personal character, and to the honourable
nature of that connection which united her to the
Heir to the Throne.

The reader will have seen, in Mrs. Fitzherbert's narration to Lord Stourton, her anxiety to secure to herself the education of the orphan daughter of Lady Horatia Seymour, committed by that lady on her death-bed to her charge. Though assented to by the Marquis of Hertford, the legal guardian, it was opposed by Lord Euston and Lord Henry Seymour, on the plea that the religion of Mrs. Fitzherbert disqualified her for having the charge of a Protestant child. On the hearing of the case in the Court of Chancery, Mr. Romilly, for Mrs. Fitzherbert, "insisted that there could be no danger to the religion of the child by the influence of Mrs. Fitzherbert." He observed, "That the residence with Mrs. Fitzherbert would not only be the means of her fortune accumulating by the time of her coming of age, but that she would derive peculiar advantage from the patronage and protection of the Prince of Wales."

The Attorney-General (the Hon. Spencer Percival), for Lord Euston and Lord Henry Seymour, commenced his speech by observing that "Mrs. Fitzherbert merited everything that could be said in her praise ; but whatever amiable qualities she might possess, the religion she professed excluded her from the right to retain the custody of a Protestant child."

Here we observe the advocate of a Lady notoriously

at the time living with the Prince of Wales as his. Wife, urging this very plea on the Lord Chancellor as a qualification for the guardianship of a female Ward; whilst the opposing counsel, objecting, indeed, to the religious opinions of Mrs. Fitzherbert, so far from questioning the arguments of his opponent, founded on the intimacy between that Lady and the Prince of Wales, adds to its force by himself bearing testimony to her meriting everything which could be said in her favour.

The opinion of the Lord Chancellor was sufficiently shown by his decision in favour of Mrs. Fitzherbert. If further proof be wanted, it may be found in the decision of the House of Lords, which, on appeal, confirmed to Mrs. Fitzherbert the education of this female charge. The part which the Prince himself took in openly avowing his interest in securing to Mrs. Fitzherbert this object of her wishes, sufficiently testified to the truth of Mr. Romilly's arguments, that the custody of that lady necessarily implied the patronage of the Prince of Wales.

As a proof of the active interest taken by the Prince of Wales to secure the attendance of Peers on the Committee of the House of Lords, to whom the question of guardianship had been referred, Mr.

Howard, of Corby, has made me the following communication :—

" Corby Castle, Jan. 20, 1856.

" DEAR MR. LANGDALE,

" In accordance with your wish I send you a copy of
the letter of the Prince of Wales to the late Charles,
Duke of Norfolk, which came into my father's hands as
his Grace's executor.

" It evinces the active interest taken by the Prince
at that period in a question which Mrs. Fitzherbert had
much at heart—namely, the fulfilment of the dying
request of her friend Lady Horatia Seymour.

" Yours sincerely,

" PHILIP H. HOWARD."

" MY DEAR DUKE,

" I have seen Lord Hertford, who will call upon you
in the course of the day, or, at any rate, before the
business is brought before the Committee.

" I am ever, my dear Duke,

" Your very sincere friend,

" GEORGE P."

" Carlton House, Monday Morning,
" Jan. 8, 1808."

The Committee of the Lords referred to sat to

consider whether or not Mrs. Fitzherbert should be entrusted with the care and education of the infant and orphan daughter of Lady Horatia Seymour, who, on her death-bed, had commended her child to Mrs. Fitzherbert's protection. The Committee decided in the affirmative, and the charge of the infant was on that day made over by her guardian and uncle, Lord Hertford, to Mrs. Fitzherbert.

Is it possible to consider the course of these proceedings, and doubt the opinion held by all the parties alluded to, as to the position in which the character of Mrs. Fitzherbert stood with regard to the respect or esteem of the public? A lady of rank and high family connections has an only child, and that child a daughter; reduced to the brink of the grave by a long-continued illness, she would, before she left this world, commit this precious relict to the charge and affection of some one who could supply to her infant daughter all that a mother, at such an hour, would select for the guardian of her child. Lady Horatia Seymour must have been intimately acquainted with the relations subsisting between her friend Mrs. Fitzherbert and the Prince of Wales. On the brink of the grave she commits, with her dying breath, her infant, a female, to the custody of this well-

known friend. Could the most perverted imagi-
nation conceive a conduct so devoid of every
parental feeling, as for a mother to surrender the
charge, the education of a daughter, to one whose
conduct could only taint the morals of her child,
did the reproach exist which has been so recklessly
brought forward against this lady of her choice ? But
supposing all this possible, and that friendship had
superseded a mother's dying anxiety for her child's
welfare, I appeal, from this parental oblivion, to the
cooler perception of legal acuteness ; and I ask, if
Lord Holland's finger of scorn could fairly have been
pointed at the relationship between Mrs. Fitzherbert
and the Prince, is it conceivable that the Attorney-
General should not have demurred to the advocacy
of Mr. Romilly, when making this very connection an
argument for the guardianship of the infant ?

That the Attorney-General was not insensible to the
importance of the moral influence that would be exercised by the guardianship of Mrs. Fitzherbert, is sufficiently evident by the very ground of his objection to
it, namely, that she was a Catholic, and as such unfit
to educate a Protestant child. Is it conceivable, then,
that the infinitely stronger ground of an immoral connection should have been passed over in silence by this

learned opponent of Mrs. Fitzherbert's claim, had he imagined that any ground for such a charge existed? It does appear to me conclusive as to the public feeling of the day, on the nature of this openly-avowed relationship between the parties, who were well known to be mutually exerting themselves for the success of the motion. Certainly the decision of the Lord Chancellor and of the House of Lords sanctions, with irresistible authority, the whole force of Mr. Romilly's arguments in favour of the beneficial guardianship of Mrs. Fitzherbert.

However gratifying to the feelings of Mrs. Fitzherbert the result might have been, which gave her the custody of a child towards whom she entertained all the attachment of a parent, the consequences of the very exertions made by the Prince to secure to her this object of her wishes, led to circumstances as destructive on other grounds of her future happiness, as the charge of her little ward had been gratifying to her almost maternal feelings.

But enough has been said on this subject by Mrs. Fitzherbert herself, in pointing out to her friend Lord Stourton the severe trials she had to endure from him who had pledged his word, and, therefore, his honour, to say the least, " her to love and to cherish."

But I will not trust myself with portraying the conduct of the plighted husband of this much-injured Wife, beyond what is actually requisite to show forth the character of her whom I have undertaken to justify in all the relations she bore to the Prince of Wales, later King George the Fourth. And on this ground I am bound to point out, not only the justification which this Lady received at the hands of others, and especially from those most intimately related by blood to the Prince and King, but also the peculiarity of the conduct of this Royal Person himself, who, whilst violating all the duties of a husband towards a wife, still seemed earnest in exacting all the claims that the most faithful of husbands could hope for.

It would appear that, however renouncing the bonds which might impose obligations upon himself, he still felt that they were binding upon Mrs. Fitzherbert, and entitled him to expect sacrifices from her which only proved, that, in spite of injuries, there was a bond between them upon which he thought he could still depend, under trials that any less sacred tie than the Marriage vow would have snapped asunder. Why assure Mrs. Fitzherbert that he would marry again, but that, notwithstanding his resolves, he still had a sense of duty which he could not shake off ? How often, in the ordinary walks of life, does the declaration of some determination of misconduct only prove the coercing tie of some torturing sense of duty, that profligacy would fain assure itself did not exist, but which even the most callous cannot altogether cast off?

What does all this prove, but that the Prince could not, even had he wished, treat Mrs. Fitzherbert as the passing favourite of a day; and that, however he might wrestle with his better feelings, a voice, "small and still," perhaps, but yet audibly, said, "She is your wife."

Certainly, one of the most peculiar proofs of this still-abiding respect is the confident demands made upon the judgment of this lady, even after his affections had been estranged. In a question of the nicest delicacy, in which he might well feel that his future character as a reigning Sovereign was at issue, he appears to have resumed the authority of a husband in his demand upon the counsel of a wife, even when his pledge had already deprived him of the power of profiting by its wisdom.

It is, indeed, difficult to understand the motive of the Prince, at that time become Regent, in requiring the opinion of Mrs. Fitzherbert on so important a step as that of the choice of the political party to which he should commit the government of the country, especially when he had already bound himself by promises to the course which he was to pursue. It is only another proof of the struggle, by which his better feelings prompted him to fall back upon that confidence, which experience had taught him could not be misplaced in her whom in a day of emergency he still remembered as his wife. The account given of the effect produced by her arguments on the Prince Regent shows the habitual influence which Mrs. Fitzherbert must have exercised over his mind. How impossible to suppose all this compatible with the sentiments entertained towards a cast-off paramour! How true a proof of the power retained by a wife over the better feelings of a husband, however passion may have robbed her of the kindlier sentiments which were her due!

History has already avenged the slighted counsels of this sensible woman; and the political events of the day would but too apparently point to the successful intrigues of the favourite over the more honest principles of the Wife. Were I to select another instance of the bold remonstrance of the Wife, listening to the dictates of duty over the risk of offence, I would refer to the appeal made to the Prince, and, I fear, made in vain, to adopt a more parental affection towards

his child, the Princess Charlotte. How affecting the
claims of this almost abandoned child on Mrs. Fitzherbert's interference to win for her a father's
love !

The question of how far this now universally-
admitted ceremony of Marriage might, or might not,
if proved at the time, have legally affected the succession of the then Prince of Wales to the throne of
this kingdom, has not unfrequently been discussed, and
certainly not been decided in the negative. By the
Statute of William and Mary, commonly called the
Bill of Rights, it is enacted, among other causes of
exclusion from the throne, that "every person who
shall marry a Papist shall be excluded, and for ever
be incapable to inherit he crown of this realm."
In such cases "the people of these realms shall be
and are hereby absolved of their allegiance." Under
this Act, the Heir Apparent would, by such Marriage
as is now admitted by all to have taken place, have
forfeited his right of succession to the throne. On the
other hand, however, it was said, that he could have
been exempted from this serious penalty of his
Marriage by the operation of the Royal Marriage
Act (12 George III.), which rendered null and void
any marriage contracted by an descendant of George

the Second, without the previous consent of the King, or a twelvemonth's notice given to the Privy Council.

By this Act it would certainly appear, that, as far as the Statute could effect it, the marriage of the Prince of Wales would have been nullified, and the issue of any such marriage would have been deemed in law illegitimate. But, still, many have maintained, that it would not, on that account, have exempted him from the forfeitures incurred by marriage with a Catholic. Indeed, it is sufficiently evident, that in many cases, where a penalty is attached to a transaction, the nullity thereof neither does affect nor ought to affect the penal consequences.

In case of bigamy, as an instance, however null the second marriage, it would be idle to argue that, on such account, the felony had not been committed, nor the just punishment incurred. The offence, in such case, consists, according to its legal description, in marrying, or contracting marriage, and the proof of this constitutes the guilt of the party—of course, irrespective of any validity. That the Prince of Wales was fully aware of this, can hardly be doubted, or that he was not prepared, even at such risk, to satisfy all the conditions on which alone he could hope to make Mrs. Fitzherbert, in her own estimation, and that of her Church, his Wife. It has appeared in her narrative that, in a moment of alarm, she tore off the names of the witnesses from the certificate of her Marriage, and the cause may have been apprehension that such an act would, if brought forward and proved, have exposed them to the pains and penalties of a *premunire*.

That such questions were much discussed at the period when they occurred, there can be no doubt, and not the least remarkable of the pamphlets of the day was one by the notorious Horne Tooke, who, treating the Statute of 12 George III. with not unusual contempt, spoke of Mrs. Fitzherbert as "both legally, really, worthily, and happily for this country, Her Royal Highness the Princess of Wales."

Whatever might have been the conduct of the Prince of Wales himself towards Mrs. Fitzherbert, it is not a little remarkable, that it did not interrupt those kind feelings with which she was regarded by almost every member of the Royal Family. Even George III. and his Queen were so far from being exceptions to this rule, that they appear, throughout her connection with their son, and even after that son's Marriage with the Princess Caroline, to have treated her with that marked respect and affection which evi-

denced, more than words could have done, their conviction of some closer tie than that arising from any
ordinary friendship towards a mere subject, however
otherwise favoured.   There is, indeed, convincing proof
that the alliance between this lady and their son, so
far from having anything demoralising in it, had a
character with which even a parent could not but
sympathise.   I have before alluded to the knowledge
which the Queen probably had of the Marriage of the
Prince with Mrs. Fitzherbert from her own son himself.   The late Mr. Weld, of Lulworth Castle, related
an anecdote of Queen Charlotte, in which it is asserted
she said to her son, before his marriage with the
Princess Caroline of Brunswick, " It is for you, George,
to say whether you can marry the Princess, or not."

The more than ordinarily friendly intercourse which
existed between Mrs. Fitzherbert and the Duke of
York for many years, partakes of all the character
of a brother towards a sister ; and worthily was this
footing of confidence exerted for all that such a
relationship could be supposed to have of beneficial
influence for the two Royal Brothers.

One of the peculiarities in this long-continued intimacy of Mrs. Fitzherbert with Royalty, and one in
which she differs, indeed, from the proverbial conduct

of Court favourites, is the perfect disinterestedness with which she acted, whether with reference to herself, or any of her relatives or friends. Acquainted as she was with all the political events which so eminently distinguished the period of her long life in public, powerful as must have been any appeal from her to the many possessors of political power during this long course of years—indeed anxious as one great leader of his party was to propitiate her offended honour—she appears to have rejected all overtures to the exertion of political influence. Conscious of her own rectitude, demanding all the respect from others which she had a right to feel for herself, she disdained any other advantages from the position in which she was placed. These, indeed, gave her rights which she could not, and would not, yield; and for the support of these she looked to him from whom she felt she had a claim to exact them. When these were at length denied her, in that quarter where they were justly due to her, she retired into that comparative privacy in which she spent the latter years of her life.

The reader will have seen in this Narrative the last effort of a virtuous wife to afford to a dying husband the consolation which all the pride and pomp of state can so little supply at that period, when the prince and

the peasant are alike to pass from their grandeur or
their poverty to the final receptacle of both—the grave.
The recorded insulting conduct of the Prince Regent,
the apparent oblivion of the King, could not make
Mrs. Fitzherbert forget the obligations contracted to
the Prince of Wales.

Could there have been a redeeming trait in the
character of this Prince and King, it might have been
in a sense of this touching conduct of a virtuous
woman, ready to encounter, under a sense of duty, all
the attendants upon a death-bed scene, painful even
though it were that of a monarch. How painful that
of George the Fourth, with all its moral and physical
accompaniments! But it was not to be! That yet
there was a lingering recollection of past years, perhaps the most consolatory for the reflection of this
King, there does appear reason to believe—perhaps
I may say hope—if contrasted with the long career
for good or evil which had elapsed since his last part-
ing with this estimable woman. The reader will have
seen Mrs. Fitzherbert's account as to the delivery of
her token, and that either some revived affection, or
some pang of remorse, attended its reception. However that may be, I have evident proof that the belief
expressed by her, that a miniature picture was sus-

pended round the neck of the King and buried with him, was correct. The King appeared to have been possessed of three portraits of Mrs. Fitzherbert. At his death, only two of these could be found; and though his gracious successor on the throne, King William the Fourth, promised his best exertions to restore the third, as well as the two others, to Mrs. Fitzherbert, it never was found. I have this well-founded account, that the third resemblance of her to whom George the Fourth had, in his early years, been so devotedly attached, was, in fact, suspended from his neck at his death, and with him committed to the grave.

It appears that Mrs. Fitzherbert had, in her correspondence with the late Cardinal Weld, expressed her strong conviction, that George the Fourth had requested he should be buried with that portrait round his neck. This correspondence had been communicated by the Cardinal to his brother-in-law, then at Rome, Charles Bodenham, Esq., of Rotherwas. This gentleman subsequently communicated the following results of his inquiry on this subject:—" It so happens, that my family were particularly intimate with the late Dr. Carr, Dean of Hereford, who was subsequently translated to the bishopric of Chichester, and then to Worcester. He was very kind and friendly with me; and, when at Worcester, I always called at the Palace. Mrs. Fitzherbert having been my wife's aunt, I had always felt *much interest* in getting at *the truth* of her history; and knowing, from the public journals, that the Bishop had attended the King (George IV.) in his last illness, I alluded to what I had heard about the portrait. It was the last interview I ever had with Dr. Carr. He had lost his wife and his favourite daughter, was himself very ill, and, as it struck me, in a very declining state. On my mentioning the name of Mrs. Fitzherbert, he said, ' Oh! she was very amiable—my faithful friend! Yes, it is very true what you have heard : I remained by the body of the King when they wrapt it round in the cere-cloth, but before that was done, I saw a portrait suspended round his neck—it was attached to a little silver chain.' The Bishop seemed exceedingly overpowered, and I took an opportunity to leave the room soon after. I went into the next apartment, where I *immediately* wrote down in my pocket-book the *very words* he had used, and the above is the exact copy."

This account strongly corroborates the display of feeling which Mrs. Fitzherbert was assured attended the reception of her letter, and certainly proves that in these last moments of King George the Fourth, sentiments were revived in the mind of the dying Monarch, which we could wish to have attended him during life, and to have been a guide to its course.

I am not, indeed, prepared to deduce much from the moral perceptions of this Sovereign; but at such a time, when about to quit the scenes of his human state and sink into the tomb, I can give no other interpretation to these last acts of his earthly career, than a confirmation of that bond which had cemented him, even in his own conscience, to a virtuous wife. It would, indeed, be a libel, even on the memory of George the Fourth, to admit, that the feelings which dictated this wish, to carry with him into the next world the recollections of his union with Mrs. Fitzherbert, could be other than such as would be accepted as righteous at that tribunal before which he was about to appear.

Such, then, was the dying testimony borne by the Royal Husband to the honourable character of his relationship in his own estimation with her whose image he desired to carry with him into his grave. But if this departed King had long deferred the recognition of a wife's claim upon his support and distinction, the

generous Monarch who succeeded him on the throne
was more sincere and more ready to acknowledge
Mrs. Fitzherbert in the relationship which she had
borne to his deceased brother.

The account which Mrs. Fitzherbert's narrative
gives of her communication with William the Fourth
at Brighton, on the one hand proves that sense of her
own rights which she had, as far as depended upon
herself, asserted during the life of George the Fourth;
on the other hand, the readiness with which King
William the Fourth at once admitted them, and acted
upon them as soon as made acquainted with them,
by having the circumstances of the Marriage, and the
documents connected with it, laid before him, authorising Mrs. Fitzherbert to wear weeds for the departed
Monarch as for her husband, desiring her to adopt
the Royal livery, advancing to receive her visit even to
the door of her carriage, practically prove what were
the sentiments of the then reigning Monarch, as to
the alliance between this lady and his late Royal
Brother. William the Fourth continued the same
kind attentions to Mrs. Fitzherbert, whenever occasions offered, as long as he lived.

The health of this interesting and distinguished
lady was rapidly declining. She spent the latter part

of her days almost entirely at Brighton, and died there
in March, 1837. There she was buried in the Catholic
Church, and a handsome monument to her memory
was erected by the Honourable Mrs. Lionel Dawson
Damer, whom we have before alluded to as the
orphan daughter of Lady Horatia Seymour, confided
by her to the guardianship of Mrs. Fitzherbert. The
inscription is as follows :—" In a vault near this spot,
are deposited the remains of Maria Fitzherbert. She
was born on the 26th July, 1756, and expired at
Brighton on the 29th of March, 1837. One, to whom
she was more than a parent, has placed this monument to her revered and beloved memory, as a
humble tribute of her gratitude and affection."

The hand of the figure had the singular addition of
three rings on the fingers, thus bearing the evidence of
the affectionate lady who erected it, to the triple marriage of her departed friend. We have, on our opening page, recited the connection of Mrs. Fitzherbert
with the family of the Welds, of Lulworth Castle,
and we only notice this connection here, to contradict a most absurd story told in the "Memoirs of
George the Fourth."* "It is worthy of notice, that

* "Memoirs of the Life and Reign of George the Fourth," by
H. E. Lloyd, Esq.

the brother-in-law of Mrs. Fitzherbert, who inherits the estate of her first husband, has recently been raised to the dignity of a Cardinal, if not precisely through British influence, yet not improbably in some measure out of compliment to His Majesty. This is a circumstance that hereafter will furnish matter for history."

I hope and imagine not; for certainly nothing could be more unfounded. The Cardinal Weld was not the brother-in-law of Mrs. Fitzherbert. This author further says:—

" Mrs. Fitzherbert is now in her seventy-fifth year, and resides at Brighton, in the enjoyment of the annuity of 10,000*l.* settled on her by the Prince."

This is again a mistake, the annuity was only 6000*l.*

Mrs. Fitzherbert's second husband, who has also been named, lost his life in consequence of his exertions during Lord George Gordon's riots. Being much heated, he bathed, and brought on the malady which soon after occasioned his death. The present possessor of Swynnerton Park, and the twenty-sixth in succession as Lord of the Manor of Norbury, is Thomas Fitzherbert, Esq., the nephew of Mrs. Fitzherbert; his father, Basil Fitzherbert, succeeding to the estates after the death of his elder brother.

I have now concluded the details upon which I confidently ground the right of Mrs. Fitzherbert to such respect and esteem as, indeed, she has invariably received from all who knew her, or who are acquainted with the circumstances connected with her Marriage. I have shown that, under no ordinary trial, she fled from her home and country, to avoid the persevering attentions of the Prince of Wales; that she then only consented to return when a Marriage according to the laws of the Church was to be the condition under which she became the wife of the Prince.

I have shown that the Prince himself claimed for her, as such, reception from his mother the Queen, and that the Royal relatives of the Prince, including both the King and Queen, universally treated her with a kindness and attention, which marked, more than words could have done, the character of the connection between her and their son.

I have shown the conscientious appeals of this upright woman, in a case of peculiar delicacy, to the authority of the Church, for guidance in her difficulty. And the closing act of her dying husband I have brought as evidence, that though a human law might have declared the act of Marriage null, yet, in the

sight of God and his conscience, he bore his dying
testimony to its validity and its truth.

In fine, the succeeding Monarch avowed his con-
viction of· the Marriage, and owned and honoured
Mrs. Fitzherbert as the widow and relict of his
Royal Brother.

And now what is to become of the packet of reserved papers at Coutts's Bank? Their existence is
not disputed, their object is avowed, under the united
testimonies of the Duke of Wellington, the Earl of
Albemarle, and Lord Stourton. They were reserved
as testimonies to the honourable relationship borne by
Mrs. Fitzherbert to George the Fourth, and as such I
have stated their nature. The details, indeed, have
been withheld by the legal possessor of them, and
however I may differ in opinion with him on the
propriety of so doing, I am far from wishing in the
slightest degree to impugn his motives.

Whether the publication of these pages may
induce the actual possessor of the papers to give to
the public, or to myself, any insight into their
particular terms and details, rests with himself.
I cannot, however, but think with a writer in the
Quarterly Review, alluding to the contents of the
sealed box, that "now that its existence is revealed,

it will not, we suppose, in these inquisitive times, be much longer withheld." If such was the opinion of the reviewer, when he still appeared perplexed between the extraordinary story of Lord Holland's Memoirs, and the plain and contradictory circumstances of the Marriage, I think, after all the circumstances which this Memoir will supply, I may safely conclude with the same reviewer, "that, after what has passed, we do not foresee any serious mischief from telling the whole truth, whatever it may be."

ILLUSTRATIONS.

DEBATES IN THE HOUSE OF COMMONS IN RE-
LATION TO THE CONNECTION OF HIS ROYAL
HIGHNESS THE PRINCE OF WALES WITH MRS.
FITZHERBERT.

" ON the 20th day of April, 1787, previous to the opening of the
Budget, a subject was brought forward in the House of Commons by Mr. Alderman Newnham, which had for some time
before strongly engaged the attention and feelings of the public—namely, the embarrassed state of the finances of the Prince
of Wales. Our readers will be pleased to recollect, that the
establishment of His Royal Highness's household took place
upon his coming of age, in the year 1783, during the administration of the Duke of Portland. It is well known, that a
great difference of opinion subsisted at that time between the
great personage with whom the final settlement of the affair
rested, and the persons whose duty it was to give him their
advice upon the subject, respecting the sum to be allowed for
that purpose. Upon a full consideration of what was thought
becoming the credit of the nation, and the exalted rank of the

Heir Apparent to the Throne, the great increase in the value of every article of expenditure, and the economy of such a liberal provision as might totally supersede the necessity of incurring debt, the Ministers of that day are said to have proposed, that an annual income should be settled upon him by Parliament of £100,000. This proposition is said to have been not only entirely disapproved of by the King, but rejected with expressions of such marked resentment, as to make the immediate resignation of those Ministers more than probable. In this emergency the Prince of Wales, who had early manifested a favourable opinion of that party, interposed, and gave the world, upon this his first step in public life, a striking proof both of filial duty and public spirit. He signified his desire, that the whole business should be left to the King; and declared his readiness to accept of whatever provision the King in his wisdom and goodness might think most fit; and, at the same time, he expressed his earnest wishes, that no misunderstanding should arise between the King and his then Ministers, on account of any arrangement in which his personal interest only was concerned. In consequence of this interference, the affair appears to have been accommodated, and an allowance of £50,000 a year, payable out of the Civil List Revenue, was settled upon His Royal Highness.

"A very few years' experience made it but too manifest, that this provision was inadequate to the purpose for which it was designed. In the year 1786 the Prince was found to have contracted a debt to the amount of about £100,000, exclusive of £50,000 and upwards expended on Carlton House. Without presuming to make any reflections upon this debt, we cannot avoid doing justice to the subsequent conduct of His Royal Highness. He was no sooner acquainted with the embarrassed state of his affairs, and the great distress in which it necessarily involved a considerable number of his creditors, than he came to a resolution of taking some effectual measures for their relief.

" His first application was to the King his father, upon whose affection alone he wished to rely, and to whose judgment he declared his readiness to submit his past and to conform his future conduct. By His Majesty's directions, a full account of the Prince's affairs was laid before him; but (whether it was from any dissatisfaction with those accounts, or with any other parts of the Prince's conduct, or from some other cause, has not transpired) a direct refusal to afford him any relief was conveyed to His Royal Highness through one of his principal officers of state.

" In consequence of this refusal, the Prince of Wales appears to have conceived himself bound in honour and justice to have recourse to the only expedient that was now left him. His determination was prompt and manly. The day after he received the message from the King, he dismissed the officers of his Court, and reduced the establishment of his household to that of a private gentleman; he ordered his horses to be sold, the works at Carlton House to be stopped, and such parts as were not necessary for his personal use, to be shut up.

" From these savings an annual sum of £40,000 was set apart, and vested in the hands of trustees for the payment of his debts.

" This conduct, however laudable it may appear, did not escape censure. It was represented, especially by the followers of the Court, as precipitate, and disrespectful to the King; and was said to have been a principal cause of that distance which, unhappily, has too long and too manifestly subsisted between them. An event, which happened soon after, afforded a public proof of the displeasure he had incurred—we mean the danger to which His Majesty's life was exposed in the month of

August, 1786. Upon that occasion no notice whatever of the accident was conveyed to the Prince of Wales by the Court— he learned it at Brighthelmstone from the information of a private correspondent. He immediately flew to Windsor. He was received there by the Queen, but the King did not see him.

"It was impossible that the situation, to which the Heir Apparent to the Throne was reduced, should be regarded with indifference either at home or abroad; and what made the indignity of his condition the more generally felt and lamented was, that no man was ever more highly qualified by distinguished affability, amiable manners, and a noble and liberal disposition, to adorn the splendour to which his exalted birth entitled him. It is reported, that the Duke of Orleans, the richest individual in Europe, who was at this time upon a visit to this country, pressed him in the strongest manner to make use of his fortune, till some favourable change should take place in his circumstances, to whatever extent he might find necessary. This offer, though doubtless generously intended, yet full of danger in its possible tendency to the public welfare, the Prince of Wales, from a nice sense of duty to the public, declined. The same public principle withheld him also from availing himself of those resources which the usurious speculations of monied men are well known to keep constantly open in this nation for the temporary wants of the necessitous.

" It was in these circumstances of private distress and public spirit, that the expedient was suggested to His Royal Highness, by several respectable members of the House of Commons, of appealing to the justice and generosity of the nation in Parliament. To this measure the Prince appears to have assented, not more from a natural wish to free himself from his pecuniary embarrassments, than from a desire to do away any bad impression, that the misfortune of having incurred the Royal displeasure, and the consequent refusal of affording him any relief, might have left upon the minds of the public.

" Accordingly, on the day already mentioned Mr. Alderman Newnham demanded, in his place, of the Chancellor of the Exchequer, whether it was the intention of His Majesty's Ministers to bring forward any proposition for rescuing the Prince of Wales from his present embarrassed and distressed situation ? For though his conduct, under the difficulties with which he laboured, reflected the highest honour upon his character, yet he thought it would bring indelible disgrace upon the nation, if he were suffered to remain any longer in his present reduced circumstances.

" To this question Mr. Pitt replied, that it was not his duty to bring forward a subject of the nature which had been mentioned, except by the command of His Majesty. It was not necessary, therefore, that he should say more, in answer to the question put to him, than that he had not been honoured with such a command. Upon this Mr. Newnham gave notice of his intentions to bring the subject regularly by a motion before the House on the fourth day of May.

" In the meantime the friends of the Prince of Wales were indefatigable in their endeavours to procure the support of the independent members of Parliament to the proposed motion; and at several meetings, which were held for that purpose, their numbers were so considerable, as to give cause of serious alarm to the Minister. On the 24th of April, Mr. Pitt, after requesting that Mr. Newnham would inform the House more particularly of the nature of the motion he intended to make, adverted to the extreme delicacy of the subject; and declared that the knowledge he possessed of many circumstances relating to it made him extremely anxious to persuade the House, if possible, to prevent the discussion of it. Should, however, the honourable Member persist in his determination to bring it forward, it would be absolutely necessary to lay those circumstances before the public; and however distressing it might prove to him as an individual, from the profound respect he had for every part of the Royal Family, he should discharge his duty to the public, and enter fully into the subject. At the same time Mr. Rolle, an adherent of the Minister, who distinguished himself greatly by his zeal upon this occasion, declared, that the question involved matter by which *the Constitution, both in Church and State,* might be essentially affected; and that if the friends of the Prince of Wales persisted in their attempt, it would be necessary to inquire into those circumstances also.

"What the circumstances so solemnly adverted to by Mr. Pitt in this conversation were, the House was left, for the present, to conjecture. The menace thrown out by Mr. Rolle was well known to allude to some supposed connection between the Prince and Mrs. Fitzherbert, a lady of a very respectable Roman Catholic family, to whom he had for some time manifested a strong attachment. For, notwithstanding the possibility of a Marriage between those two parties was effectually guarded against by the Royal Marriage Act, great pains had been taken, and not entirely without success, to mislead the ignorant, and to inflame the minds of the vulgar upon that subject; with what view, it would have been more easy to conceive in former times than at present, when all the enemies of the House of Brunswick are supposed to have ceased from amongst the nation.

"On the 27th of the same month Mr. Newnham, in compliance with the request that had been made, signified to the

House that the motion he intended to make would be to the following effect, 'That an humble Address be presented to His Majesty, praying him to take into his Royal consideration the present embarrassed state of the affairs of the Prince of Wales, and to grant him such relief as his Royal wisdom should think fit, and that the House would make good the same.'

"Several members on both sides of the House having risen to deprecate the further discussion of this business, and to express their earnest wishes that it might be accommodated in some other manner, Mr. Sheridan got up to declare, that the insinuations and menaces, which had been thrown out upon a former occasion, made it impossible for the Prince to recede with honour.   He said he had the highest authority to declare, that His Royal Highness had no other wish, than that every circumstance in the whole series of his conduct should be most minutely and accurately inquired into; that no part of his conduct, circumstances, or situation, should be treated with ambiguity, concealment, or affected tenderness, but that whatever related to him should be discussed openly, and with fair, manly, and direct examination; and that he was ready, as a Peer of Great Britain, to give in another place the most direct answers to any questions that might be put to him.

"Mr. Rolle observed, in reply, that he had acted and should act as it became an independent country gentleman to do, when the dearest interests of the nation were at stake, from the conviction of his own mind; and that if the motion proposed was persisted in, he should state without reserve his sentiments upon the subject he had alluded to, according as the matter struck him.

"Mr. Pitt declared, that he had been greatly misunderstood, if it was conceived that he meant to throw out any insinuations injurious to the character of the Prince of Wales. The particulars to which he alluded, and which he might find it necessary to state fully to the House, related only to his pecuniary affairs, and to a correspondence which had taken place on that subject, and which he thought would satisfy the House of the impropriety of complying with the proposed motion.

"On the 30th Mr. Newnham rose again, to make a few observations upon what had passed on Friday preceding. He remarked, that much had been said of the tenderness of the ground upon which he trod, and of the dangerous consequences that might arise from his perseverance. He declared himself totally ignorant of the grounds of those apprehensions, with which others were so unaccountably filled. If there was danger in the measure, let those who gave occasion to it tremble at the consequences. He saw none: the Prince saw none: and it was by his express desire that he now gave notice that he should pursue his design. Highly honoured, as he conceived himself to be, by the Prince's confidence upon this occasion, he was not to be intimidated; and he could assure the House, that neither was His Royal Highness to be deterred from his purpose by the base and false rumours which were spread abroad concerning him.

"Mr. Fox, who had been absent on the former debate, came down this day with immediate authority from the Prince of Wales, to assure the House there was no part of his conduct that he was either afraid or unwilling to have investigated in the fullest manner. With regard to the private correspondence alluded to, he wished it to be laid before the House, because he could take upon himself to assert, that it would prove the conduct of His Royal Highness to have been in the highest degree amiable, and would present as uniform and perfect a picture of duty and obedience, as ever, in any instance, had been shown from a son to his father, or from a subject to his Sovereign. With respect to the debt, which was the cause of his present difficulties, the Prince was willing, if the House should deem it necessary, to give a fair and general account in writing of every part of it; and if any suspicion should exist, that this or that general article might comprehend sums of money improperly applied, he would give a clear explanation of the particulars to His Majesty, or to his Ministers. Lastly, with respect to allusions made by one member, to something full of *danger to the Church and State*, he wished he had spoken more explicitly. If he alluded to a certain low and malicious rumour, which had been industriously propagated without doors, he was authorised to declare it to be a falsehood. He had thought that a tale fit only to impose upon the lowest of the vulgar, could not have gained credit for a moment in that House, or with any one who possessed the most ordinary portion of common sense and reflection; but when it appeared that an invention so gross and malicious, a report of a fact which was actually impossible to have happened, had been circulated with so much industry and success, as to have made an impression upon the minds of the members of that House, it both proved the uncommon pains taken by the enemies of the Prince of Wales to depreciate his character and injure him in the opinion of his country, and ought to be a caution to the House, and to the nation at large, how they gave credit to any other scandalous and malignant reports that were circulated to his prejudice.

" Mr. Fox concluded with adding, that he was further authorised by His Royal Highness to declare, that he was ready, as a Peer of Parliament, to answer in the other House any the most pointed questions that could be put to him respecting this report, or to afford His Majesty or his Ministers any other assurances or satisfaction they might require.

" Mr. Rolle replied, that he was not singular in his fears for the Church; other gentlemen had been equally alarmed; and he should be happy to find that their apprehensions were groundless. The right honourable Member had said, that the fact alluded to was impossible to have happened. They all knew, indeed, that there were certain laws and Acts of Parliament which forbade it, and made it null and void; but still it might have taken place, though not under the formal sanction of law; and upon that point he wished to be satisfied.

" Mr. Fox observed, that though what he had said before was, he thought, sufficient to satisfy every candid and liberal mind, he was willing, if possible, to satisfy the most perverse. When he denied the calumny in question, he meant to deny it, not merely with regard to the effect of certain existing laws, but to deny it *in toto*, in point of fact as well as law. The fact not only never could have happened legally, but never did happen in any way whatsoever, and had from the beginning been a base and malicious falsehood.

" Mr. Rolle rose again, and desired to know, whether what Mr. Fox had last said, was to be understood as spoken from direct authority?

" Mr. Fox replied, that he had direct authority.

" It appears to have been expected, that upon this declaration Mr. Rolle would have expressed his full satisfaction; and being called upon by a member so to do, he said that nothing should induce him to act otherwise than to his own judgment should seem proper. An answer had certainly been given to his question, and the House would judge for themselves of that answer.

" This conduct occasioned some warm reflections from Mr. Sheridan and Mr. Grey, who said, that the Member, after having put a pointed question for the solution of doubts existing in his own mind, and having received an immediate answer, was bound in honour and fairness either to declare that he was satisfied, or to take some means of putting the matter into such a state of inquiry as should satisfy him. To remain silent, or to declare that the House might judge for itself, was neither manly nor candid: it tended to aggravate in a high degree the malicious falsehood which had been propagated, by admitting a supposition, that the Prince might authorise a false denial of the fact.

" Mr. Pitt defended Mr. Rolle with great warmth, and declared, that what had been said by the members who preceded him was the most direct attack upon the freedom of debate, and liberty of speech in that House, that he had ever heard since he sat in Parliament.

" Mr. Rolle stated shortly the part he had taken; declared that he had been induced so to do by his affection for the Prince; that he had not said he was unsatisfied; and that he left the whole to the judgment of the House.

" The favourable impression which this debate, the open and manly conduct of the Prince, and the harshness with which he had been treated in his most private and personal concerns, left upon the minds of men both within and without the doors of Parliament, appears to have given the Minister a serious apprehension, that upon the question itself he might be left in a minority."—*Annual Register,* 1787.

MR. MOORE'S ACCOUNT OF THE DISCUSSION IN
PARLIAMENT WITH RELATION TO THE CON-
NECTION OF HIS ROYAL HIGHNESS THE
PRINCE OF WALES AND MRS. FITZHERBERT.*

" Mr. Sheridan, who was now high in the confidence of the
Prince, had twice, in the course of the year 1786, taken occasion to allude publicly to the embarrassments of His Royal
Highness. Indeed, the decisive measure which this illustrious
person himself had adopted, in reducing his establishment and
devoting a part of his income to the discharge of his debts,
sufficiently proclaimed the true state of affairs to the public.
Still, however, the strange policy was persevered in, of adding
the discontent of the Heir Apparent to the other weapons in
the hands of the Opposition;—and, as might be expected,
they were not tardy in turning it to account. In the spring of
1787, the embarrassed state of His Royal Highness's affairs
was brought formally under the notice of Parliament by
Alderman Newnham.

"During one of the discussions to which the subject gave
rise, Mr. Rolle, the member for Devonshire, a strong adherent
of the Ministry, in deprecating the question about to be agitated, affirmed that 'it went immediately to affect our Constitution in Church and State.' In these solemn words it was
well understood that he alluded to a report at that time generally believed, and acted upon by many in the etiquette of
private life, that a Marriage had been solemnized between the
Prince of Wales and Mrs. Fitzherbert, a lady of the Roman

* "Memoirs of the Life of the Right Hon. Richard Brinsley Sheridan."

Catholic persuasion, who, with more danger to her own peace than to that of either Church or State, had for some time been the distinguished object of His Royal Highness's affection.

"Even had an alliance of this description taken place, the provisions of the Royal Marriage Act would have nullified it into a mere ceremony, inefficient, as it was supposed, for any other purpose than that of satisfying the scruples of one of the parties. But that dread of Popery, which in England starts at its own shadow, took alarm at the consequences of an intercourse so heterodox : and it became necessary, in the opinion of the Prince and his friends, to put an end to the apprehensions which were abroad on the subject.

"Nor can it be denied that, in the minds of those who believed that the Marriage had been actually solemnized,* there were, in one point of view, very sufficient grounds of alarm. By the Statute of William and Mary, commonly called the Bill of Rights, it is enacted, among other causes of exclusion from the throne, that ' every person who shall marry a Papist, shall be excluded, and for ever be incapable to inherit the Crown of this realm.'—In such cases (adds this truly revolutionary Act) ' the people of these realms shall be, and are hereby, absolved of their allegiance.' Under this Act, which was confirmed by the Act of Settlement, it is evident that the Heir Apparent would, by such a Marriage as was now attributed to him, have forfeited his right of succession to the throne. From so serious a penalty, however, it was generally supposed he would have been exempted by the operation of the Royal Marriage Act (12 George III.), which rendered null and void any Marriage contracted by any descendant of

"* Horne Tooke, in his insidious pamphlet on the subject, presumed so far on this belief as to call Mrs. Fitzherbert ' Her Royal Highness.' "

George II. without the previous consent of the King, or a twelvemonth's notice given to the Privy Council.

"That this Act would have nullified the alleged Marriage of the Prince of Wales there is, of course, no doubt;—but that it would have also exempted him from the forfeiture incurred by marriage with a Papist, is a point which, in the minds of many, still remains a question. There are, it is well known, analogous cases in law, where the nullity of an illegal transaction does not do away the penalty attached to it.* To persons, therefore, who believed that the actual solemnization of the marriage could be proved by witnesses present at the ceremony, this view of the case, which seemed to promise an interruption of the succession, could not fail to suggest some disquieting apprehensions and speculations, which nothing short, it was thought, of a public and authentic disavowal of the Marriage altogether would be able effectually to allay.

"If in politics princes are unsafe allies, in connections of a tenderer nature they are still more perilous partners; and a triumph over a Royal lover is dearly bought by the various risks and humiliations which accompany it. Not only is a lower standard of constancy applied to persons of that rank, but when once love affairs are converted into matters of state, there is an end to all the delicacy and mystery

---

"* Thus, a man by contracting a second marriage, pending the first marriage, commits a felony; and the crime, according to its legal description, consists in marrying, or contracting a marriage—though what he does is no more a marriage than that of the Heir Apparent would be under the circumstances in question.

"The same principle runs through the whole law of entails both in England and Scotland, and a variety of cases might be cited, in which, though the act done is void, yet the doing of it creates a forfeiture."

which ought to encircle them. The disavowal of a Royal
Marriage in the Gazette would have been no novelty in
English history;* and the disclaimer, on the present occasion, though entrusted to a less official medium, was equally
public, strong, and unceremonious.

"Mr. Fox, who had not been present in the House of Commons when the member for Devonshire alluded to the circumstance, took occasion, on the next discussion of the question,
and, as he declared, with the immediate authority of the Prince,
to contradict the report of the Marriage in the fullest and most
unqualified terms :—it was, he said, 'a miserable calumny, a
low malicious falsehood, which had been propagated without
doors, and made the wanton sport of the vulgar;—a tale, fit
only to impose upon the lowest orders, a monstrous invention,
a report of a fact which had not the smallest degree of foundation, actually impossible to have happened.' To an observation from Mr. Rolle, that 'they all knew there was an Act of
Parliament which forbade such a Marriage; but, that, though
it could not be done under the formal sanction of the law,
there were ways in which it might have taken place, and in
which that law, in the minds of some persons, might have been
satisfactorily evaded,'—Mr. Fox replied, that 'he did not deny
the calumny in question merely with regard to certain existing laws, but that he denied it *in toto*, in point of fact as well
as of law :—it not only never could have happened legally, but
it never did happen in any way whatsoever, and had from the
beginning been a base and malicious falsehood.'

"Though Mr. Rolle, from either obstinacy or real distrust,
refused, in spite of the repeated calls of Mr. Sheridan and

"* See in Ellis's 'Historical Letters,' vol. iii., the declarations of Charles
II. with respect to his marriage with 'one Mrs. Walters,' signed by himself, and published in the *London Gazette*."

Mr. Grey, to declare himself satisfied with this declaration, it was felt by the Minister to be at least sufficiently explicit and decisive, to leave him no further pretext, in the eyes of the public, for refusing the relief which the situation of the Prince required. Accordingly, a message from the Crown on the subject of His Royal Highness's debts was followed by an addition to his income of £10,000 yearly out of the Civil List; an issue of £161,000 from the same source, for the discharge of his debts; and £20,000 on account of the works at Carlton House.

"In the same proportion that this authorised declaration was successful in satisfying the public mind, it must naturally have been painful and humiliating to the person whose honour was involved in it. The immediate consequence of this feeling was a breach between that person and Mr. Fox, which, notwithstanding the continuance, for so many years after, of the attachment of both to the same illustrious object, remained, it is understood, unreconciled to the last.

"If, in the first movement of sympathy with the pain excited in that quarter, a retractation of this public disavowal was thought of, the impossibility of finding any creditable medium through which to convey it, must soon have suggested itself to check the intention. Some middle course, however, it was thought, might be adopted, which, without going the full length of retracting, might tend at least to unsettle the impression left upon the public, and in some degree retrieve that loss of station which a disclaimer, coming in such an authentic shape, had entailed. To ask Mr. Fox to discredit his own statement was impossible. An application was, therefore, made to a young member of the party, who was then fast rising into the eminence which he has since so nobly sustained, and whose answer to the proposal is said to have betrayed some of that unaccommodating highmindedness, which, in more than one collision with Royalty, has proved him but an unfit adjunct to a Court. The reply to his refusal was, 'Then, I must get Sheridan to say something;' and hence, it seems, was the origin of those few dexterously unmeaning compliments with which the latter, when the motion of Alderman Newnham was withdrawn, endeavoured, without in the least degree weakening the declaration of Mr. Fox, to restore that equilibrium of temper and self-esteem, which such a sacrifice of gallantry to expediency had naturally disturbed. In alluding to the offer of the Prince, through Mr. Fox, to answer any questions upon the subject of his reported marriage, which it might be thought proper to put to him in the House, Mr. Sheridan said—'That no such idea had been pursued, and no such inquiry had been adopted, was a point which did credit to the decorum, the feelings, and the dignity of Parliament. But whilst His Royal Highness's feelings had no doubt been considered on this occasion, he must take the liberty of saying, however some might think it a subordinate consideration, that there was another person entitled, in every delicate and honourable mind, to the same attention; one, whom he would not otherwise venture to describe or allude to, but by saying it was a name which malice or ignorance alone could attempt to injure, and whose character and conduct claimed and were entitled to the truest respect."

SIR W. WRAXALL'S ACCOUNT OF THESE TRANSAC-
TIONS IN HIS " POSTHUMOUS MEMOIRS OF
HIS OWN TIME."

" *May*.—London presented during the spring of 1786 a
scene of general dissipation at the West End of the town. All
the gloom which the disasters of the American War had diffused
during successive years over the capital, seemed to have dis-
persed like a dream. The Prince of Wales, then in the prime
of youth, led the way in every species of pleasure, and in many
species of excess. His father, aware of the injury which such
an example might produce among the younger branches of his
family, had early removed his second and third sons from England : Prince Frederic being sent, in December, 1781, to Hanover; while William Henry, bred to the navy, pursued his
professional career at a distance from his native country. Mrs.
Fitzherbert, commonly regarded, if not as the Heir Apparent's
wife, yet as united to him by a ceremony substituted in place of
a legal Marriage, received in all companies the consideration and
respect which the sanctity of such a supposed connection was
calculated to inspire.

" I have already mentioned that she was in her second
widowhood when she became known to him. It is a curious
fact, that Edward the Black Prince espoused a lady who,
like Mrs. Fitzherbert, had previously given her hand to two
husbands. ' The Fair Maid of Kent,' as she was denomi-
nated, mother of Richard the Second, stood in that predica-
ment. There appears, indeed, to have been among the Kings,
and in the Royal Family of England, an extraordinary predi-
lection for widows. Not to mention the unfortunate consort

of Edward the Fourth, and Henry the Eighth's last Queen; the three uncles of the Prince of Wales all, either avowedly or secretly, acted the same part. I know that Lady Mary Coke considered herself united to Edward, Duke of York (who died in 1767 at Monaco), by as legitimate a union as the Duchesses of Gloucester or of Cumberland were united to their respective husbands. She was, indeed, much higher born than Miss Walpole or Miss Luttrell, being daughter of John, the celebrated Duke of Argyle, and she possessed extraordinary personal beauty. At more than seventy years of age, when I have been in company with her, she preserved the cheerfulness and vivacity of youth.

"*20th April.*—The attention of Parliament, and of all England, was suddenly diverted at this time into a new channel, by the debts of the Prince of Wales; which, within the space of less than four years, were become intolerably oppressive to himself. All application to the Sovereign for assistance being found ineffectual, it was determined by his secret advisers, at whose head presided Lord Loughborough, Fox, and Sheridan, to throw him at once on the generosity of the House of Commons. Alderman Newnham, who, in the course of the preceding session, when the subject of His Royal Highness's pecuniary embarrassments was agitated, had expressed his conviction that the income of the Heir Apparent could not be found adequate to the support of his dignity, was again selected on the present occasion. He possessed neither the eloquence nor public consideration which seemed to qualify him for so delicate an office; but, as one of the representatives for the City of London, he might be supposed to speak the sentiments of his constituents. Newnham, addressing himself across the table to the Chancellor of the Exchequer, requested to be informed, whether it was the intention of Ministers to bring forward any proposition for rescuing the Prince of Wales from his very distressed situation. He added, that the question thus asked did not originate in personal curiosity; as, according to the nature of the answer returned, he might find it expedient to ground a Parliamentary proceeding. Pitt, thus interrogated, replied very laconically, that it not being his duty to open such a subject, except by command of His Majesty, it was only necessary for him to say that he had received no such directions. The Alderman then gave notice, that on the 4th of the ensuing month he would propose to the consideration of the House a *motion* relative to the Prince of Wales. Here terminated the conversation.

" *24th April.*—Public curiosity being universally excited by the expected agitation of a question in which the King and his eldest son must form the two opposite parties, and which might in its progress give rise to the most painful disclosures, Pitt endeavoured, about four days later, either wholly to avert it, or, if that should be found impracticable, at least to ascertain the nature of the intended *motion*. Rising for the purpose, after alluding to the delicacy of the subject itself, he expressed a wish to know whether the honourable magistrate still persisted in forcing it forward on the attention of the House. 'If he retained his determination,' the Minister added, 'at least its scope and tendency ought to be stated.' Newnham replied that *he* did not *force forward* a discussion, which was propelled by its own weight; that he had not yet decided on the precise form in which he should vest his proposition; but that its object would be to rescue the Prince of Wales from his actual pecuniary difficulties. The Minister sarcastically observing, that it was singular to have given notice of a *motion*, without previously determining what it should be, especially as it regarded a matter of such gravity and novelty,

Fox came forward to Newnham's assistance. Having concurred in the *latter* part of Pitt's observation, Fox subjoined his hopes that, on account of the necessity which would arise for investigating the causes of His Royal Highness's distress, the business itself might be anticipated, and some act performed which must supersede the proposed *motion*. 'I admit,' answered the Chancellor of the Exchequer, 'the necessity of investigation; and precisely for that reason, combined with my profound respect for the illustrious family concerned in it, I would, if possible, prevent discussion. The information which I possess on the point, renders me peculiarly desirous of avoiding it; but, if a determination should be manifested to bring it before this assembly, I shall, however distressing it may be to myself as an individual, discharge my public duty by entering fully into the subject.'

"*27th April.*—These reciprocal menaces soon led to more determined indications of hostility. Newnham having announced that his intention was 'to move an Address to the Throne, entreating His Majesty to inquire into the Prince's embarrassed situation, and to rescue him from it;' Rolle, who, though he furnished in his own person matter for political and poetic ridicule, yet represented a great county; and who, however coarse in his language he might be, wanted not intelligence or firmness in the discharge of his Parliamentary duties, instantly expressed his disapprobation of the proposed *motion*. 'It is,' continued he, 'a proposition which tends immediately to affect our Constitution, *both in Church and State*. If, therefore, it should ever be brought forward, I will, as soon as the honourable magistrate sits down, move *the previous question;* —for I am decidedly of opinion that it ought not to be discussed within these walls.' Fox being absent on that evening (not, as he afterwards declared, premeditatedly, with a view of

avoiding the mention of such a topic, but because he was
unacquainted with the intention to agitate it),—Sheridan took
on himself to justify the appeal to Parliament. 'A county
member,' exclaimed he, 'stands forward, and calls on the
country gentlemen to aid him in opposing a discussion which
may affect our Constitution *in Church and State*. The subject
is doubtless in itself momentous: but dark insinuations have
been thrown out, in order to magnify its importance. They
have even been used as arguments to deter His Royal Highness's
friends from introducing any measure likely to produce an
inquiry into his conduct, under the penalty of disclosing
alarming facts. I am, however, confident, and I speak from
authority, when I assert that he wishes every part of his conduct to be laid open, without ambiguity or concealment. Such
is the unequivocal reply which the illustrious personage would
himself give, as a Peer of Parliament, if this subject should
ever be agitated in another assembly.'

"Not in the least degree intimidated by Sheridan's speech,
Rolle replied that no man present felt more loyalty towards his
Sovereign, or towards the Heir Apparent, than himself. 'Nevertheless,' added he, 'if a *motion* is proposed, which I hold
to be improper, I shall act as becomes an independent country
gentleman. *I expect nothing from His Majesty nor from his
successor.* I will therefore fulfil my duty, by opposing a proposition which may produce serious *differences* between the
father and the son.' The sincerity of this concise and lofty
declaration of disinterestedness, worthy of *Andrew Marvel*, or
of *Shippen*, must yet be liable to some sort of doubt; since,
only nine years afterwards, the member for Devon kissed hands
at St. James's, on being raised by Pitt to the British Peerage.
And it is difficult to suppose, that even at the time when he
professed so much indifference to the honours which emanate

from the Throne, he had not in view to obtain a seat in the Upper House.

"Various persons now interposed, to deprecate the further discussion of so momentous a question. Among them Powis rose, who, however elevated might be his motives, nourished in his bosom a systematic ambition, not incompatible with an ardent desire of promoting the public welfare. In urgent terms he implored of Newnham not to prosecute his threatened intention; adding, that he ought to entreat permission to withdraw his notice. But Sheridan instantly appealed to the Chancellor of the Exchequer, whether, by adopting such a course, the Prince would not seem to concede to terror, what he had refused to argument. Under these circumstances, the Minister, after again expostulating both with Newnham and with Sheridan, on the impropriety of persisting to bring forward a proposition big with public mischief, finding all his efforts for preventing it fruitless, contented himself with declaring, that the particulars to which he had alluded during a former debate, as necessary to be stated by him to the House, related solely to a correspondence which had taken place respecting the pecuniary embarrassments of the Prince, and had no reference to any *extraneous facts*.

"*30th April.*—Fox, who, as I have already observed, had not been present at this debate, attended in his place when the subject was resumed, and performed the principal part; speaking in the name, and by the immediate authority, of the Heir Apparent. Mrs. Fitzherbert formed, in fact, the prominent object of inquiry, though she was not brought to the bar, and personally interrogated, as we have beheld another female treated in 1809.

"Fox having expatiated on the hardship of the Prince of Wales's situation, and declared His Royal Highness's readiness to state every particular of the debts which he had incurred, next adverted to Rolle's allusion. Without naming any individual, he stigmatised the report itself as 'a low malicious calumny, destitute of all foundation, impossible ever to have happened, and propagated with the sole view of depreciating the Prince's character in the estimation of the country.' Rolle readily admitted its *legal* impossibility, but he maintained that there were modes in which it might have taken place. He added, that the matter had been discussed in newspapers all over the kingdom, impressing with deep concern every individual who venerated the British constitution. Fox replying, that he denied it in point of *fact*, as well as of *law*, the thing never having been done in any way, Rolle demanded 'whether he spoke from direct authority?' To this question Fox answered decidedly in the affirmative; and here the dialogue terminated.

"Neither the Chancellor of the Exchequer, nor any other member present, took part in it; silence pervading the House, which, as well as the gallery, was crowded to the utmost degree. Mrs. Fitzherbert being now disclaimed as the wife of the Prince of Wales, in the most formal terms, by a person who came expressly commissioned for the purpose, on behalf of the personage principally interested, and Rolle making no reply, a sort of pause ensued; the debate, as far as it regarded the supposed matrimonial union or contract in question, seeming to be at an end.

"Such would probably have been the fact:—for Fox, satisfied with exposing the falsity of the imputation, never once opened his lips during the remainder of the discussion. But Sheridan, who always manifested an aversion towards Rolle, observed that, after the explicit answer given on the present occasion, it would be most unhandsome in the member for

Devon not to express his satisfaction. Finding, nevertheless, that no disposition was manifested to comply with his demand, Rolle simply remarking, that he had certainly received an answer, and that the House must form their own opinion of its propriety, Sheridan returned with more personality to the charge. 'Such a line of conduct,' he said, 'was neither candid nor manly; and the House ought therefore to resolve it seditious, as well as disloyal, to propagate reports injurious to the character of the Prince of Wales.' Rolle, however, refused to concede, or to declare any conviction on the subject. 'I did not invent these reports,' he answered, 'but I heard them, and they made an impression on my mind. In order to ascertain how far they had any foundation, I put the question; and in so doing, I am convinced that I have not acted in an unparliamentary manner.'

"The Chancellor of the Exchequer, who, during the course of Rolle's interrogatory to Fox, had not interposed, now rose, and with great animation arraigned Sheridan's proceeding, as the most unqualified attack which he had ever witnessed on the freedom of debate. 'Those,' added Pitt, 'who exhibit such warmth on the present occasion, ought rather to acknowledge their obligation to the individual who has suggested a question which produced so explicit a declaration on this interesting subject :—a declaration which *must* give complete satisfaction, not only to him, but to the whole House.'

"Rolle's tenacity in withholding his assent to the satisfactory nature of Fox's answer, was equally displayed by Sheridan, on Pitt's attempt to force from him the avowal. With uncommon ingenuity he endeavoured to demonstrate, that Rolle, having received an explicit denial of his insinuation, was bound either to admit his error, or to adopt measures for discovering the

P

truth. 'It would,' continued he, 'be aggravating the malicious falsehood circulated, to assert that the Prince of Wales had authorised a false denial of the fact. Even the Minister himself is obliged to *assume* that the honourable Member *must be satisfied*, as he has not had sufficient candour to make the acknowledgment.' Thus pressed, Rolle once more rose, and after observing that his affection for the Heir Apparent dictated the question put by him, added, 'The honourable gentleman has not heard me say I am *unsatisfied*.' Grey vainly endeavoured by a repetition of Sheridan's arguments, couched in still more intemperate language, to elicit from Rolle a less equivocal recognition. But Pitt, indignant at the expressions used by Grey, repelled his attempt with great warmth. While the Chancellor of the Exchequer disclaimed every idea of menace, he persisted to declare that all those to whom the harmony and the happiness of the Royal Family were dear, ought to join with him in deprecating the threatened discussion; or, if it could not be prevented, at least to give it the most decided opposition. 'No possible necessity,' concluded he, 'can be pleaded for recurring to this assembly on a subject which in propriety, as well as in decency, ought to originate with the Crown; since I know that *there exists no want of becoming readiness in another quarter, to do everything which ought to be done in the business.*' With this declaration, which seemed, if it was improved, to open a door for mutual concession, the debate closed; each party professing a determined intention of trying the issue, and both sides anticipating a favourable result."

Woodfall and Kinder, Printers, Angel Court, Skinner Street, London.